Now you are a
PRINCIPAL

PRAISE FOR *NOW YOU ARE A PRINCIPAL*

This insightful book masterfully weaves real-life scenarios and case studies to illustrate the multifaceted responsibilities of a principal and CEO. Through its authentic and detailed narratives, it offers a profound understanding of the challenges and complexities faced by educational leaders. The book not only serves as a practical guide but also encourages readers to reflect on their own practices, providing a structured framework to critically evaluate one's readiness to step into a principal role. It stands out as an essential read for all aspiring leaders, offering both inspiration and practical advice for navigating the demanding landscape of educational leadership.

William Campbell, Founding Head, Franklin School, USA

This book resonated closely with my own experiences as a current principal. Dr Teys communicates in a way that brings the reality of the lived experience to life, giving a genuine sense of the many joys, challenges and emotions that are faced each day. Dr Teys eloquently highlights what is at the very core of the role, offering practical advice and wisdom from his vast experience in leading schools with impact from the 'head and the heart'.

Scott Donohoe, Principal, Catherine McAuley Catholic College, Medowie, NSW

Paul's insights into being a school leader offer more than just a practical guide. The book has the effect of placing a new leader in the passenger's seat, allowing them to view through the windscreen the highs and lows of an experienced leader's journey. It was definitely NOT written from a distant, theoretically-based, academic stance, and yet it stands as an erudite read that can guide neophyte leaders. It's a book that will become dog-eared through use.

Phil Roberts, Principal, Mount Sinai College, Sydney, 1990–2023; professional coach, mentor and problem solver

Now you are a
PRINCIPAL

*Navigating the
leadership labyrinth*

DR PAUL TEYS

Copyright © Paul Teys 2024

All rights reserved. No part of this book may be reproduced or transmitted in any form or by any means, electronic or mechanical, including photocopying, recording or by any information storage and retrieval system, without prior permission in writing from the publisher.

Published by Amba Press
Melbourne, Australia
www.ambapress.com.au

Editor – Andrew Campbell
Cover Designer – Tess McCabe

ISBN: 9781923215283 (pbk)
ISBN: 9781923215290 (ebk)

A catalogue record for this book is available from the National Library of Australia.

CONTENTS

Acknowledgements		ix
Introduction		1
Chapter 1	The visionary compass	5
Chapter 2	Building the dream team *Effective staff recruitment and development*	23
Chapter 3	The culture conundrum *Shaping and sustaining school culture*	55
Chapter 4	Navigating the seas of change *Change management and innovation in education*	81
Chapter 5	Managing the board	99
Chapter 6	Managing sticky situations and stakeholders	121
Chapter 7	The balancing act *Managing resources and priorities*	139
Chapter 8	Crisis leadership *Responding to challenges and emergencies*	155
Chapter 9	The ethical compass *Ethical decision-making and integrity*	167
Chapter 10	Achieving work–life harmony as a principal	175
Chapter 11	Passing the torch *Succession planning and leaving a legacy*	191
Conclusion		203
References		205

ACKNOWLEDGEMENTS

Writing a book is a journey that extends beyond the author alone, and this book has been no exception. I am profoundly grateful to a number of people whose support and contributions have been invaluable.

First, my heartfelt thanks to Melanie Ward for being a critical friend, advocate, and unwavering supporter throughout this process. Melanie's insights and feedback as the first major reviewer were instrumental in shaping this book.

I must also extend my gratitude to Alicia Cohen of Amba Press. Alicia's exceptional work in publishing my first book was a significant motivation for me to embark on writing this sequel. Her professionalism and dedication have made our collaboration a true pleasure.

To the dedicated principals who reviewed my manuscript amidst their incredible workloads, your perspectives and suggestions have added immense value to this book. Your willingness to engage with this project has enriched its content significantly.

Lastly, I am grateful to everyone who purchased my first book, *So You Want to Be a Principal*. Your encouragement and positive feedback have not only inspired me but have also fuelled my passion for continuing to write.

Thank you all for your part in this journey.

INTRODUCTION

In the ever-changing landscape of education, the role of a school principal stands as a cornerstone of dynamic leadership and profound understanding. Spanning over four decades in schools, my journey has been rich and varied, encompassing 24 years as a principal across four schools in three different states. This book captures those experiences, an exploration of my leadership, my personal and professional journey. It is more than a compilation of leadership strategies; it is a trek through the various dimensions of educational leadership aimed at enriching and empowering current and future school principals, aspiring principals, and leaders.

It is a narrative that examines what it means to lead, inspire, and manage an educational community. This is my journey, a playbook for those who aspire to shape the future of school communities. As a principal in various schools across three states, my career has been a testament to the belief that leadership is about more than managing – it is about envisioning, inspiring, and nurturing.

"Do not go where the path may lead, go instead where there is no path and leave a trail". This quotation, often attributed to Ralph Waldo Emerson, resonates deeply with the core of this book. Throughout my time in independent schools, which saw all but four years in leadership roles, I have sought to carve untravelled paths, setting a precedent for innovative and transformative leadership. Each chapter of this book is a testament to my leadership journey, guiding current and aspiring principals on navigating the multifaceted aspects of leadership in schools.

This is a book about possibilities. It is about harnessing the raw potential of educational spaces and transforming them into centres of excellence. From conceptualising a vision that unites and excites to navigating the complexities of school governance, each chapter is crafted to help you explore the depth and breadth of school leadership. With a blend of personal anecdotes and practical advice, I invite you to join me in redefining what it means to lead in education.

Beyond the technicalities of management, this book dives into the art of leadership. It is about the nuanced balance of aligning a school's vision with the heartbeat of its community, the delicate equilibrium of driving innovation while honouring tradition, and the bold act of leading through times of turbulence with integrity and grace. It is about the human side of leadership – the relationships, the challenges, and the moments of triumph.

As you turn these pages, you will find yourself equipped with strategies and the wisdom to use them astutely. Whether you are stepping into principalship for the first time, an aspiring principal or looking to deepen your existing practices as a principal, this book is a companion for your journey – a guide to show the way as you navigate the rich and rewarding path of educational leadership.

In my years as a teacher, leader, and principal, I have come to understand that the crux of educational leadership transcends the boundaries of conventional management. It is an amalgamation of vision, empathy, and resilience. Each challenge faced, whether in curriculum innovation or crisis management, taught me that leadership is less about directives and more about dialogue, understanding, and adaptability. Through this journey, I have seen firsthand how a leader's actions, big or small, ripple through the entire school community, crafting a narrative that extends far beyond the school's walls. This book is an invitation to explore these narratives to understand that at the heart of educational leadership lies the power to shape not just schools, but futures.

In my decades at the helm of a variety of schools, I have learned that the heart of leadership lies not in the grandeur of titles but in the quiet moments of connection and the bold decisions made in the face of uncertainty. Each school I served was a unique ecosystem, a medley of ambitions, challenges, and triumphs, and it was my role to nurture this environment, guiding it towards a future that was as ambitious as it was attainable.

Navigating the complexities of budget constraints while advocating for the best resources taught me the delicate art of financial stewardship in education. I learned the importance of transparent communication with the community, ensuring that every stakeholder felt heard and involved. Facing crises, be they natural disasters or public health concerns, underscored the significance of composed and ethical decision-making. These experiences shaped not just the schools I led but also myself, as a leader and a lifelong learner.

One of the most profound lessons I have gleaned is that leadership in education is as much about listening as it is about leading. In the corridors and classrooms, in the common room, and in the midst of sports fields and music halls, the voices of students and teachers alike echoed the true needs and aspirations of the school. Whether it was adapting to the evolving educational landscape, integrating technology into the curriculum, or fostering an inclusive culture, each decision stemmed from an understanding that a school is a community first.

I vividly recall the uncharted paths of my journey, where maps were yet to be drawn and I relied on my core values and my team's collective wisdom to guide me. Navigating the school through financial challenges demanded tough but compassionate decisions, while other times called for pioneering, bold educational programs. Rooted in real-life experiences and practical tools, this narrative aims to assist aspiring principals. As you explore these pages, I hope they offer strategies, insights, and inspiration to help you carve your own path in the noble field of educational leadership.

In my tenure as a principal, I have learned that educational leadership is an intricate labyrinth, woven with the threads of vision, empathy, resilience, and innovation. It is about creating an environment where every student finds their rhythm and every teacher feels valued and empowered. I recall championing initiatives that seemed daunting but were crucial for holistic growth – like integrating technology into our curriculum or fostering inclusive practices that celebrated diversity within our school community.

This book encapsulates my learnings, offering insights into the multifaceted role of a principal, through the eyes of a veteran school principal. It is a journey through challenges and triumphs, aiming to guide and inspire current and future educational leaders towards creating impactful and enduring legacies in their schools.

CHAPTER 1

THE VISIONARY COMPASS

1.1 Introduction

In discussing the concept of "vision" in leadership, it is crucial to differentiate between a school's formal "vision statement" – a succinct declaration that encapsulates the school's overarching aspirations – and the dynamic and multifaceted implementation of this vision through various initiatives. A vision statement is typically a concise articulation, serving as a standard-bearer that guides all strategic planning and decision-making. It reflects the core identity and long-term objectives of the institution.

However, the spirit of vision in a leadership context extends beyond this formal statement. It encompasses the various strategic initiatives that actualise the vision statement in the daily life of the school. For instance, the examples I use in this chapter, the introduction of an International Baccalaureate (IB) program or the construction of a new music hall, are not isolated visions but tangible manifestations of the school's commitment to fostering a comprehensive and globally competitive educational environment. These projects illustrate how a leader translates a static vision statement into dynamic and impactful actions that resonate with the entire school community.

Each initiative, while distinct, should be seen as a thread in the larger representation of the school's vision, contributing to a cohesive narrative that advances the school's fundamental goals. This approach to vision emphasises that leadership is not just about setting a direction but also about embodying and implementing the vision in every facet of school operation. It invites a broader interpretation of vision as an ongoing, living process that adapts to new challenges and opportunities, always aligned with the school's core values but flexible in its execution.

Thus, when we talk about a leader's "visions", we refer to the specific, actionable plans that bring the formal vision statement to life, ensuring that it is not merely a static slogan but a living, breathing reality that impacts every member of the school community.

1.2 Navigating the vision

At the heart of transformative school leadership lies a compelling vision – a standard-bearer that guides decisions, shapes goals, and inspires the school community to strive for excellence. It is the foundation upon which the school's future is built and a crucial element that distinguishes outstanding schools from merely good ones.

A vision in the educational context goes beyond mere aspiration; it articulates the values and principles that a school stands for and depicts the future it seeks to create. It serves as a roadmap for progress, providing a clear direction for all stakeholders. When effectively communicated and shared, a vision can unite teachers, students, and parents in a common purpose, fostering a strong and collaborative school culture.

As a principal, crafting a vision for my school(s) began with deep introspection and a comprehensive understanding of the community's needs. I went about identifying what makes our school unique and envisioning how it could serve our students better – not just academically but as global citizens of tomorrow. It required forecasting educational trends, anticipating future challenges, and proposing innovative solutions.

But a vision is not just an idealistic dream; I was deliberate in ensuring it was grounded in reality. It must be actionable, with clear objectives that can be broken down into strategic plans and tangible outcomes. This balance between the aspirational and the practical gives a vision its power – it motivates and mobilises, yet it also sets a standard for accountability and measurable progress.

From my experience as a principal, developing a vision was a participatory process. I engaged with my executive leaders to brainstorm possibilities, with teachers to understand their perspectives, listening to students to appreciate their aspirations, and collaborating with parents to recognise their hopes for their children's education. I involved the board at appropriate times for their input and review of ideas that were bubbling to the surface. This inclusive approach enriched the vision with diverse viewpoints and fostered a sense of ownership across the school community.

For instance, when we aimed to incorporate Moodle (https://moodle.org/), an eLearning platform, into our curriculum, it wasn't solely about adopting new technology; it was about fostering an adaptable and interactive learning environment. Our vision was to harness Moodle's capabilities to enhance student engagement, facilitate personalised learning, and support collaborative educational experiences.

Through town hall meetings, surveys, and discussion forums, we shaped a vision that teachers, students, and parents saw value in, making it a collective ambition rather than a top-down initiative. By involving the school community in this process, we built a shared commitment to integrating Moodle effectively, ensuring that it would enrich our educational offerings and equip our students with the skills for a digital future. Our director of information technology exemplified effective leadership and communication, fostering a strong collaborative environment with teachers and leaders. This is why he was successful:

- **Accessibility.** He maintained an open-door policy, making himself readily available to staff for support, discussions, and feedback. This approach not only made him approachable but also facilitated a two-way communication channel that was both responsive and welcoming.
- **Educational resources.** Understanding the varying levels of tech proficiency among staff, he developed concise, two-minute instructional videos. These bite-sized resources allowed staff to quickly grasp new technologies and apply them without significant downtime, thereby reducing frustration and increasing adoption rates.
- **Regular updates.** By holding fortnightly briefing meetings, he kept the staff informed of the latest IT developments and upcoming projects. These regular updates ensured that everyone was on the same page and had the opportunity to discuss how changes would affect their work, promoting a culture of transparency and inclusion.
- **Educational background.** His background as a teacher was instrumental in building credibility and trust. His ability to educate and explain complex technical issues in simple terms was highly valued. This educational approach helped demystify technology, making it more accessible to all staff members.

These strategies not only improved IT operations but also reinforced a culture of open communication and mutual respect, which is essential for any thriving educational environment.

In summary, the nucleus of vision in school leadership lies in its ability to capture the collective aspirations of the school community and translate them into a roadmap for the future. A well-crafted vision charts a course for educational excellence and binds the community together, ensuring that every stakeholder contributes to the school's success story.

True educational leadership goes deeper than mere reaction to societal shifts; it involves foresight and pioneering initiatives that set the stage for these changes. For instance, by integrating forward-thinking programs like digital literacy and sustainability into the curriculum ahead of widespread adoption, we not only prepared our students for the future but also positioned our school as a leader in educational innovation. This proactive approach not only equips students with necessary skills but also establishes the school as a catalyst in shaping societal norms and expectations.

1.2 Engaging stakeholders with your vision

Transforming a school's vision into a vibrant, living ethos isn't a solitary endeavour; it is a collaborative journey that demands the involvement of all stakeholders. The key to making this vision come alive lies in securing the buy-in and collective effort of the entire school community.

In a time where change is the only constant, effective school leadership extends beyond being merely reactive to external pressures. A leader's ability to anticipate and strategically respond to upcoming challenges is crucial. For example, by engaging with a broad array of thought leadership resources, such as OECD reports, McKinsey insights, and educational podcasts, I was able to gain a wide-angled view that not only informed but also predicted and shaped my response to these changes.

This proactive approach was starkly evident in our handling of the mental health crisis within schools. Instead of the common reactive measures that often exacerbate the issue, our strategy involved a pre-emptive wellness program that integrated mental health awareness and support into the daily curriculum, thereby addressing the issue before it escalated into a crisis. This not only helped in mitigating the impact but also positioned our school as a leader in proactive mental health management.

Through such initiatives, I could transform a school from one that simply responded to changes to one that could foresee and actively manage them, thereby becoming a true catalyst of societal transformation.

In this subchapter, I will use the example of my vision for the school to become an International Baccalaureate (IB) World School (https://www.ibo.org/) to contextualise the key learnings for the reader.

My first engagement with the IB was in 2006, and at the time Australian IB schools were mainly schools offering Diploma (Year 11 and 12) programs. No Australian schools were offering all four IB programs. This was my vision, and it was revolutionary in the Australian context.

I engaged with the school's board before presenting the vision to the wider community. It was crucial to ensure that my vision aligned with the broader strategic objectives of the school and had the board's full support. After thorough consultations, the board endorsed the vision, recognising its potential to elevate our school's status as an IB school with all four programs. This endorsement was a significant milestone, establishing a strong community engagement foundation.

In our quest to turn the vision of being an IB school with all four programs into a reality, we implemented various strategies aimed at ensuring that teachers, students, parents, and the wider community weren't just aware of the vision, but were also active participants in its fulfilment.

We organised inclusive workshops and forums, providing multiple opportunities for stakeholders to convene and share their hopes, concerns, and ideas. These gatherings allowed voices to be heard, contributing significantly to shaping the school's vision to become an IB World School. As you might anticipate, not all parents were fans of the idea or familiar with the IB. I saw an opportunity to engage with these parents, give them my time, listen, and work together with them toward developing an understanding of the emphatic benefits the IB programs would bring.

Introducing the IB was pivotal in expanding our students' educational horizons, enabling them to see beyond the local region's confines and envision a global future. This initiative was crucial in fostering a broader world-view, encouraging our students to think of the entire world as their potential destination and field of opportunity.

Surveys and questionnaires played a crucial role in gathering feedback from those unable to attend in-person sessions. The data collected revealed trends and common themes that needed consideration in our vision.

Teachers at the forefront in their experience and understanding of an IB education were encouraged to participate in dedicated brainstorming sessions. I allowed them to lead. This gave them the opportunity to discuss their professional aspirations and the needs of their students, providing invaluable insights for crafting an aspirational yet practical vision. They visited other IB schools to grow their knowledge to support the journey.

We recognised the importance of parent-teacher groups as a bridge between the school and families. Their unique perspective helped align the school's vision to be an IB World School with community values and expectations. There was a strong alignment between the school's values and ethos and those of the IB.

A team of champions for the IB, consisting of representatives from across the K–12 teaching cohort, worked iteratively to craft the vision statement. They considered input from the broader community, refining the vision accordingly. The parents who had rich, positive experiences of the IB in other international contexts became our champions.

Transparent communication was maintained throughout the process, with regular updates shared via newsletters, the school website, and social media, inviting ongoing feedback from stakeholders. The IB organisation had a rich array of collateral that we could use.

Formal adoption events were held to mark the finalisation of the vision. These events, such as the exhibitions and visits by IB staff from overseas, symbolised the entire school community's commitment to the new direction.

By actively involving stakeholders in the vision-setting process, we gained a wealth of perspectives and fostered a sense of collective ownership. When everyone feels they have contributed to the vision, they are more inclined to work together towards its realisation, ensuring that the school progresses as a united and committed community. By becoming an IB World School, we not only achieved a significant milestone but also successfully implemented three out of the four IB programs by the time of my retirement, a testament to our collective dedication and transformative progress.

1.3 From abstract to action – operationalising the vision

In the heart of a school's transformative journey, where a vision becomes reality, lies a narrative of meticulous planning and collective effort. This story unfolds in the following steps.

A school's vision, much like the North Star, guides you. The example I will use here is the state-of-the-art music centre at Moreton Bay College. This vision represented more than a building; it was a vision of a vibrant hub where student dreams would find their voice.

1. **Strategic planning workshops.** The school community's collective brainstorming crystallised the vision into strategic initiatives, aligning daily work with the broader goals.
2. **Role-specific objectives.** I assigned tasks to different school community members, from the director of music, head of the development office, and teachers to administrative staff.
3. **Resource allocation.** I directed funds, time, and energy efficiently. Realisation of the centre required the injection of 25 percent of the total investment required to come from donations. This campaign in itself was huge.
4. **Prioritisation.** I ensured that every resource spent contributed to growth.
5. **Communication plan.** I kept the vision alive through updates, visual cues, and branded messaging.
6. **Curriculum and policy integration.** With the head of music, we could embed the vision in curriculum revision, targeted professional development, and policy refinement.
7. **Monitoring and celebrating progress.** We tracked success through data and stories, celebrating milestones as shared triumphs.
8. **Continuous feedback and leadership accountability.** I maintained a responsive approach to community needs and set performance goals to ensure the centre would meet the community's expectations.

I used regular community surveys, conducting periodic surveys within our community to gather insights and opinions. I would distribute these surveys through various channels such as email, social media, and mail-outs (the old days). The questions would focus on the quality of educational services that had to be provided, the effectiveness of communication from leadership, and suggestions for improvements. This direct feedback from community members helped guide the college leadership team in making informed decisions and adjustments to better meet the community's expectations and needs.

As I reflect on this chapter of my leadership journey, the music centre stands not just as a structure but as a monument to collective will and determination. I have had the pleasure of returning and listening to the melodies filling its halls, reminding me of its transformation from an abstract dream to concrete reality. With my wingman, Jeff, we created more than a centre for musical excellence; we laid the foundation for personal and artistic triumphs. This transformation should remind us all that visions are blueprints for the future, a symphony of dedication and belief in our shared dreams.

1.4 Communicating the vision

Effective communication breathes life into a school's vision, transforming it from a statement on paper into a living ethos that permeates every facet of school life. Through communication, a vision gains clarity, gathers momentum and commands a presence within the daily routine of school activities and interactions.

In the art of communicating a vision, repetition is a friend. The vision should be echoed in every corridor and classroom, not as a monotonous chant but as a chorus that rises from the genuine enthusiasm of all involved. It must be articulated in a manner that resonates, using accessible language that connects with the hearts and minds of teachers, students, and parents.

While this letter is not particularly related to communicating a vision, it is a good illustration of effective communication written from a heartfelt stance. Principals must show heart and human leadership. The letter was written to a school community when Covid-19 first hit our shores.

> *Dear Staff, Parents, and Carers,*
>
> *In times of uncertainty, the true strength of our community shines brightest. As news of the Covid-19 pandemic reaches our shores and concerns naturally arise, I want to address you all directly to offer reassurance and clarity in the midst of confusion.*
>
> *Our school has always been a pillar of stability and safety, and it is in challenging times like these that our shared vision of informed, conscious navigation through crises becomes most vital. We understand the concerns you may have about the safety and well-being of our students and staff, and I want to assure you that every decision we make is with their best interests at heart.*
>
> *We are closely monitoring the situation, following guidelines from health authorities, and adapting our actions as new information be-*

comes available. We are implementing enhanced cleaning protocols, considering adjustments to school operations, and preparing for all possible scenarios with the utmost caution and foresight.

To our dedicated staff, your health and safety are paramount. We are here to support you with clear directives and necessary resources as you continue to educate and inspire our students in these trying times.

To our students, your resilience and adaptability are qualities that will serve you well not just now, but throughout life. We are working tirelessly to ensure that your learning journey continues with as little disruption as possible.

To our parents, your partnership has never been more important. We are committed to clear and timely communication so you can make informed decisions for your family. We encourage you to maintain open lines of communication with us, share your concerns, and collaborate as we navigate this situation together.

While we may not have all the answers immediately as this global situation evolves, be assured that our leadership is informed, proactive, and deeply committed to the safety and continuity of our educational mission. We are a community that cares, and believes that strength in unity will guide us through these uncharted waters.

Let us proceed with calm, with reason, and with the knowledge that we are surrounded by a community of support. Together, we will weather this storm and emerge stronger for it.

With heartfelt solidarity and unwavering commitment ...

The principal is the vision's chief narrator, ensuring its message is captured in the narrative of every school event, newsletter, and meeting. The principal's speeches, informal chats with staff, and presentations at parent-teacher evenings all serve as channels to underscore the vision's relevance and importance. This consistent reinforcement helps the community to internalise the vision, making it a natural part of their language and thoughts.

I refer to nuance and subtle sharing of the vision, not soap-box-style oration.

But communication is not a one-way street. It thrives on interaction, inviting the school community to hear the vision and speak it back, engage with it, question it, and contribute to it. This dynamic exchange turns the vision into a dialogue, one that fosters.

1.5 Leading by example – the principal as the visionary

In a school's journey of futures thinking, vision and strategy, the principal is the compass – the visionary leader whose role transcends management duties to embody the very spirit of the school's vision. My experience taught me that it is a role that demands not just foresight and passion but the embodiment of the school's ethos in every action and decision.

I felt that when I was acting as the living exemplar of the school's values, I was sending a powerful message. It was not enough to merely craft and communicate a vision; I had to live it. This commitment to leading by example is what transformed a set of ideals into a palpable school culture. I was the first to arrive and the last to leave, demonstrating dedication. Greeting students and staff enthusiastically each day, showing that every community member is valued, was important to me in being a breathing example of the vision.

As the principal, I chose to spend lunchtimes in the cafeteria, not merely to eat but to actively oversee and engage with students, sharing in their world. This practice not only allowed me to stay connected with the student body but also facilitated informal, yet meaningful interactions that could boost student morale and provide me with insights into the school culture. When faced with budgetary constraints, I was the principal who first re-evaluated my own expenditures before asking others to do so. This approach exemplified fiscal responsibility and sacrifice, setting a leadership example that promoted a culture of integrity and accountability among the staff. By demonstrating such commitment, in both financial management and personal engagement, I influenced the overall climate of the school, encouraging teachers to also adopt a mindset of conscientious resource use and deeper involvement with students

Leading by example also meant being a visible advocate for the vision. When new initiatives were launched, I was at the forefront, not only endorsing but actively participating. Whether it was integrating technology in the classroom or promoting new teaching methodologies, my direct involvement as principal and the practical support I could give would alleviate apprehension and inspire confidence among staff.

In the heart of a region where tradition often overshadowed innovation, I embraced the role of the visionary by introducing the International Baccalaureate (IB) program to our school (see section 1.2). It was a bold move, spurred by the conviction that our students deserved a global education platform that promised to broaden their horizons and equip them for an interconnected world. My aim was to enrich our curriculum and ignite a transformation in how we viewed and valued education.

By the time I was ready to pass this vision on to my successor, I knew we had achieved that goal.

The journey was akin to planting an exotic tree in familiar soil. It required nurturing, patience, and the community's trust. As the principal, I led from the front, becoming the program's champion and conduit for its cultural shift. I worked tirelessly to weave the IB's ethos into the fabric of our school's identity, ensuring that its principles of inquiry, reflection, and open-mindedness became as much a part of our character as the regional values we held dear.

The introduction of the IB was a testament to the power of visionary leadership. It proved that even in the most unlikely places, educational excellence knows no boundaries and that with a clear vision and a steadfast leader, a school can indeed become a crucible for world-class education and innovation.

As the principal, I had to model resilience and adaptability, especially in challenging times like Covid-19, to set the tone for the school's approach to obstacles. I always believed my role was to show calm and grace under pressure, creativity in problem-solving, and a relentless pursuit of excellence. When the school community saw me, their leader, navigate difficulties with optimism and strategy, it instilled a culture of perseverance, ingenuity and trust.

However, embodying the vision does not mean perfection. It means authenticity. I had to also be transparent about challenges and open to feedback from my executive, the board, and parents. Such vulnerability invited trust and fostered a collaborative spirit within the school. My resolve was sorely tested by a board who got "itchy" feet. It was not always smooth sailing.

The concept of the principal as the visionary serves as a compass – guiding the school with clear direction and purpose. When a principal's leadership steadfastly points towards the school's vision, it legitimises that vision and energises the entire community to action. This form of leadership acts as a navigational tool, setting the course for the community and ensuring that every initiative and decision aligns with the broader goals of the institution. Such leadership cultivates fertile ground where the seeds of the school's vision are sown and nurtured, and its students are given the opportunity to grow into the leaders of tomorrow.

1.6 Vision in action – case study

In the 1990s, as the principal of Moreton Bay College, I held a vision that felt as vast as the Australian continent itself. It was a vision to establish a brother school for Moreton Bay College, a revered century-old institution dedicated to girls' education. The idea was audacious and unprecedented – to create a boys' school that would offer an education to match the esteemed learning our daughters were receiving – a feat not attempted in Australia for 70 years.

Together with a circle of visionaries, we set about turning this dream into a reality. One notable visionary and companion in the quest was Jeff Buchanan, my head of development, a personal friend and colleague. Another was a golfing buddy, Brent Hailey, who held a senior management position at a locally based yet international property development company. However, the journey was fraught with challenges that tested our resolve. Our ambitious proposal was met with significant resistance from local independent schools, which viewed our vision as a shake-up to the status quo. The political opposition was fierce; our initial application for a new school was met with rejection, casting a shadow of doubt over our aspirations.

Yet, in the face of these formidable obstacles, we found an unlikely champion. The then Education Minister, who would later rise to become the Premier of Queensland, saw the potential in our proposal. Recognising the value of providing balanced educational opportunities for both sons and daughters, the Minister became an ally in our quest. We navigated the political maelstrom with their support, advocating tirelessly for our cause.

It was a testament to the power of conviction and the might of collaboration. The Minister's backing by approving the school was the catalyst we needed; their influence opened doors that had been firmly closed, and their advocacy tipped the scales in our favour. With renewed vigour, we pressed on, and the state government's approval was secured – a triumph against the odds.

The establishment of Moreton Bay Boys' School was a victory not only for us but for the entire community. It celebrated equitable education and was a nod to the future where every child, regardless of gender, could aspire to greatness. Our vision had weathered the storm of opposition, and as the school recently turned 20, the echoes of those early challenges only served to sweeten the success.

Looking back on those times from the vantage point of two decades, I am filled with pride. The resistance we faced and the political hurdles we overcame are now part of the school's rich history, a narrative of perseverance and belief in a cause that was right and just. The boys' college is a legacy of that vision, a shining example of what can be achieved when passion for education meets the courage to challenge the status quo.

1.7 Overcoming obstacles to the vision

When I stepped into the role of head of curriculum at a venerable institution steeped in a 70-year tradition of academic rigour, I was met with a singular narrative: university as the sole indicator of post-graduation success. The school's vision was myopic, fixated on the percentage of graduates securing university spots, a metric worn like a badge of honour. However, I recognised the latent potential in diversifying student pathways – this was the heart of my leadership vision.

The resistance was palpable. Alumni bristled at the notion of alternatives to university, fearing it would dilute the school's prestigious reputation. Parents, too, were sceptical, having selected the school for its track record in university placements. Convincing them required strategic communication, highlighting the evolving job market and the value of varied educational trajectories. I organised forums featuring successful professionals from technical and vocational fields, facilitated discussions with parents, and showcased success stories of individuals who thrived outside the traditional university route.

It was the support of my principal at the time who gave me the resilience, resolve, and fortitude to keep pushing for the pathway for our students. He never retreated from his stoic stance of unequivocal backing, but he let me run with it.

Implementing this expanded vision meant reorienting the school's culture and curriculum. I began by introducing workshops focused on career diversity, embedding technical training opportunities, and integrating TAFE programs into our curriculum. I sought buy-in from teachers by demonstrating how these pathways could cater to different student strengths, thereby enhancing our educational inclusivity. Teachers came on board because they were committed to the best for their students. Once I could show the benefits to the students they cared for, they were behind me. Students joined the dialogue as they shared their hopes and aspirations with me and the careers advisor, letting us know that university was not the first choice for all students.

To sway the community, I led by example, becoming an advocate for all paths of success. I emphasised that our mission was to equip students for their future, not just for university. It was about preparing them for life, in all its varied possibilities. I celebrated every apprenticeship and traineeship with the same fervour as a university acceptance, gradually shifting the school's perception of success.

The obstacles to this vision were significantly rooted in deep-seated beliefs and traditional values. However, the key to overcoming them was persistent, empathetic dialogue and providing tangible evidence of the benefits of diverse educational pathways. Over time, the vision took hold. The school began to cherish the diversity of its graduates' paths, seeing it as a reflection of a holistic and adaptable education.

This journey taught me that a leader's vision often requires challenging the status quo, facing resilient resistance, and steering the community through the tides of change with patience and unwavering conviction. It is about painting a picture of the future, including every student's potential and celebrating each step towards that inclusive vision. In this case study, dozens of families who had never spoken up about the preoccupation with university entry as the only post-Year 12 destination found voice.

1.8 Sustaining and celebrating the vision through change and milestones

In an ever-evolving educational landscape, sustaining a school's vision is akin to steering a ship through shifting seas. This challenge requires a principal to act as both an anchor and a sail – firmly grounded in foundational values while agile enough to navigate changes. The key lies in adapting without losing sight of overarching goals, embedding flexibility into the vision's fabric, and cultivating a culture of continuous learning.

A vision should serve as a compass, allowing for navigation through educational demands while staying true to its course. This requires foresight, wisdom, and a commitment to a dynamic, living vision. Communication is crucial; revisiting the vision in meetings, information evenings, staff meetings, and annual presentation events keeps it at the forefront of the school's collective consciousness.

When I took on the role of establishing a new boys' school, we encountered not only unforeseen challenges but also well-intentioned yet distracting interference from the board. Despite these hurdles, we remained steadfast in our mission to realise a distinct vision for the school – one that aligned closely with what parents envisioned for their sons' education. These parents had expressed a clear preference for an educational approach similar to that of Moreton Bay College, rather than settling for the alternatives available in the local area.

To ensure that our school not only met but exceeded these expectations, we engaged deeply with the entire school community – parents, teachers, and board members alike. This engagement was crucial, as it helped refine our vision to ensure it was not only aspirational but also deeply relevant to the needs and hopes of our families. By actively involving parents in the conversation and decision-making process, we aligned the school's objectives with their expectations, thus making our educational model resonate more effectively with what they believed was the best for their children.

Milestones punctuate this journey, serving as indicators of progress and celebration points. Establishing them starts with defining critical achievements along the path to the vision. They should be strategically spaced and challenging, encompassing a range of objectives from quick wins to significant long-term achievements.

At one of my schools, the "One percent" initiative spearheaded by the head of teaching and learning represented a strategic, focused effort to enhance each student's academic performance. The concept was straightforward yet powerful: each teacher was tasked with identifying and implementing strategies that would help every student improve their performance by at least one percent in every subject. This was not about overwhelming students with extra work; rather, it was about making small, targeted adjustments in teaching methods, feedback, and academic support that were specifically tailored to each student's unique needs and potential.

The cumulative effect of these small improvements was profound. As each student improved slightly across various subjects, these marginal gains added up to significant overall enhancement. The initiative led to the school achieving remarkable academic success, placing it in the top 50 of the Higher School Certificate (HSC) league tables in New South Wales.

While I have always been wary of placing undue emphasis on league tables, this achievement was a strategic opportunity that we leveraged to our advantage. The recognition helped to elevate the school's reputation, attracting more students and affirming its educational strategies.

The success of the "One percent" initiative also provided a substantial boost to our marketing and promotional efforts. For years, we capitalised on this milestone, using it to highlight the effectiveness of our educational approach and the tangible benefits it brought to our students. Importantly, celebrating these achievements played a crucial role in our school community. It was an opportunity to acknowledge the hard work and commitment of both students and staff. By recognising and celebrating these incremental improvements, we reinforced our commitment to our shared vision and fostered an environment of continuous improvement.

This initiative not only improved academic outcomes but also strengthened our school community. It demonstrated how collective efforts and small changes can lead to extraordinary results, thus encouraging a culture of achievement and ongoing development that benefited everyone involved.

Celebrations should involve introspection, cyclical review and reflection, understanding what works, and learning from challenges. Recognising progress externally through newsletters and social media strengthens community bonds. As a principal, setting and celebrating milestones is a motivational tool, providing direction and a culture of cherished progress.

In conclusion, sustaining a vision through change is about leading purposefully into the future. It is about resilience, creativity, and an unwavering commitment to education as a transformative force. As principals, we should embrace the role of a gardener, tending to the vision, and adapting strategies, but always keeping the roots firmly planted. A sustained vision is not immobile but a living entity that grows and adapts over time. Remember, every step towards the vision is meaningful, telling a story of a school that dreams, acts, and achieves.

1.9 Key takeaways

As we close the first chapter of our journey through visionary leadership in education, we anchor ourselves with key takeaways from "The visionary compass". The lessons learned pave a path for aspiring leaders and principals to navigate the multifaceted responsibilities that come with the principalship.

1. **Vision as the school's heartbeat**
   - A vision sets the rhythm for all school activities, from policies to classroom lessons.
   - It should be clear, inspiring, and actionable.
   - Involve the entire school community in creating the vision for collective support and strength.
2. **Translating vision into reality**
   - Balance aspirational goals with achievable outcomes.
   - Break down abstract visions into strategic, measurable steps.
   - Set and celebrate milestones, but also use them for reflection and adjustment.
3. **Effective communication of the vision**
   - Engage in active listening and speaking.
   - Maintain open feedback channels.
   - Show the community their contributions in the evolving vision.
   - Encourage ownership through demonstration in daily actions.
4. **Leading by example**
   - Embody the vision as its champion.
   - Inspire others to adopt the vision's values and goals.
   - Ensure the vision adapts to changes while maintaining its quintessence.
5. **Handling resistance**
   - Use empathy and strategic communication when facing resistance.
   - Highlight the benefits of innovation with success stories and pilot programs.
   - Maintain transparency and conviction through challenges.
   - Stay attuned to the community's concerns.
6. **Visionary leadership**
   - Align your actions with the articulated vision.
   - Stay informed, reflective, and connected to your community.
   - Be adaptable, as a static vision is unsuitable for a dynamic educational environment.
7. **Continual learning and growth**
   - Embrace the journey of continuous learning, growth, and leadership.
   - Personalise these lessons in your leadership style.
   - Aim to create a school that inspires students to reach high and become guiding lights themselves.

CHAPTER 2

BUILDING THE DREAM TEAM
Effective staff recruitment and development

2.1 Building the team

The journey begins with identifying the right mix of people in your quest to build a dream team for a school setting. They are not merely educators with impressive résumés but those whose moral purpose resonates with the heart and soul of your school and more broadly with excellence in leadership. This narrative explores the multifaceted qualities that define an ideal team member in a school context.

Imagine walking through the halls of your school. You observe educators who are not just disseminators of knowledge but are architects of a future generation. At the core of this dynamic team are a shared vision and values. Each member, passionately aligned with the school's mission, is a source of inspiration, guiding students not just academically but holistically. This alignment with the school's ethos is the foundation of every other skill.

For school leadership, adaptability and innovation are the winds of change. The educators who stand out are those who embrace these winds. They are the ones who are not content with the status quo but are constantly seeking new horizons in teaching methodologies, technologies, and educational trends. They are restless to do better, for students. Their adaptability is not a forced trait but a natural response to the changing needs of their students.

Collaboration is the melody that plays softly in the background of this educational symphony. It is about more than just teamwork; it is a spirit that pervades every interaction, whether with colleagues, students, or the broader community. These leaders recognise that learning is a collaborative journey, and they excel at integrating their unique skills to foster collective growth.

Integrated seamlessly into the structure of this team is emotional intelligence – a quality that shines through in their interactions. It is seen in how they manage their classrooms, the empathy with which they address student concerns, and their respect and understanding towards their colleagues. This emotional acumen fosters a nurturing and inclusive environment crucial for learning and teaching.

I remember at one of my schools, when I entered the common room for my constitutional coffee, I noticed a staff member deeply engrossed in a book, not fiction, but a scholarly book about the challenges of students from rural communities adjusting to big-city boarding life. This scene was a snapshot of a continuous learner; I knew there had to be a place for her on my dream team. Her quest for knowledge was unending, and her passion for self-improvement was infectious; once on my team, she ensured that other team members remained at the forefront of educational thinking and innovation. Her hallmark was giving her colleagues books to read. Initially met with mild amusement, it quickly transformed to an insatiable appetite to read.

2.2 True leadership transcends titles

In my experience, true leadership often transcends titles and formal roles, manifesting itself in various, sometimes unexpected, forms. A vivid example of this was one of my most effective leaders, who, intriguingly, held no official title. Their leadership was not about authority or recognition but about passion and possibility. This primary school teacher was a constant presence in my office, engaging in what we fondly termed "chewing the fat" sessions – deep discussions about what could be achieved, always exploring the realms of the possible. They had a remarkable knack for never seeking credit, their satisfaction derived solely from seeing good ideas take flight and positively impact our school community.

Each Christmas, they would give me a book, thoughtfully chosen to challenge and expand my thinking. The real gift, however, came after the holidays when we would reconvene to debrief. These sessions were more than mere discussions; they were an exchange of ideas and insights, sparking inspiration and innovation in our educational approach. Their dedication to these debriefs was a testament to their commitment to growth, both personal and institutional.

Overall, this leader exemplifies how true leadership can manifest in non-traditional roles, emphasising that the foundation of leadership lies in influence, inspiration, and the ability to see and nurture potential in others. Formal leadership was bestowed on her as part of my senior team.

Here are the leadership qualities that stood out in this unintentional leader:

1. **Influence without authority.** This leader was effective without needing a formal title or traditional power structures. They led through their actions and the influence they had on others, demonstrating that leadership effectiveness is not contingent on official status.
2. **Passion and visionary thinking.** The leader was driven by passion and a vision of what could be achieved, not by the desire for recognition or credit. This shows a forward-thinking, visionary quality that focuses on possibilities and potential improvements within the school.
3. **Collaborative engagement.** Regularly engaging in deep, explorative discussions ("chewing the fat" sessions) with myself and others, this leader used collaboration as a tool to foster innovation and change. These discussions were instrumental in shaping and expanding the educational approach of the school.
4. **Humility and selflessness.** The leader's lack of concern for personal credit and their satisfaction in seeing ideas succeed reflect a humble and selfless approach. This humility in leadership is crucial for fostering an environment where everyone feels valued and motivated to contribute.
5. **Commitment to continuous learning and development.** By giving books and engaging in detailed debriefs, this leader emphasised the importance of continuous intellectual and professional growth. This quality shows a dedication not only to personal development but also to the advancement of the school's educational mission.
6. **Inspiration and motivation.** The enthusiasm and dedication to exploring new ideas and engaging in meaningful dialogues serve as inspiration to others. This leader's ability to inspire and drive innovation highlights their capacity to lead through motivation and intellectual stimulation.

This example beautifully illustrates the crux of leadership in our context. Leadership is not just about leading a classroom project, mentoring a struggling student, or spearheading a new initiative. It is about the inherent qualities that drive staff to contribute positively, regardless of their official capacity. Each member of our team, in their unique way, demonstrates the potential to lead and influence positively, mirroring the impact of the leader who walked into my office without a title but left an indelible mark on me and our school's journey. Their approach reminds us that leadership is about influence, inspiration, and the pursuit of shared goals, transcending traditional notions of hierarchy and authority.

Finally, the resilience and patience of these particular educators, destined for leadership, form the backbone of your dream team. They face challenges with a steady hand and interact with students and colleagues with an enduring patience. Their resilience is a testament to their commitment to education and their unwavering belief in the potential of their students.

The dream team in an educational setting is a collective of shared vision, adaptability, collaboration, emotional intelligence, continuous learning, effective communication, leadership, resilience, and patience. It seems almost overwhelming, but with the best leaders this is a natural part of their DNA. These qualities, when intertwined together, create a team capable not just of imparting knowledge but of shaping futures. I had the wonderful honour of leading such teams in my schools.

Recognising the strengths of each team member, I ensured that our decision-making process was genuinely collaborative. We instituted regular brainstorming sessions, allowing each member to voice their perspectives and contribute to our strategy. This approach not only enriched our decisions but also fostered a sense of ownership and commitment across the team. By sharing leadership, we could tap into a diverse array of ideas, leading to more innovative and effective solutions.

What should I look for when assembling my leadership team? Selecting the right individuals is crucial for fostering a successful and cohesive group. Here are five key attributes I consider when choosing my team members:

1. **Aligned vision and values.** I look for individuals who share the school's vision and core values. Alignment in these areas ensures that the team will work towards common goals with a unified philosophy, which is essential for maintaining consistency and integrity in decision-making.

2. **Diverse skills and expertise.** I assemble a team with a diverse range of skills and expertise to cover all necessary aspects of school management and educational leadership. Diversity in skills promotes innovative solutions and allows the team to handle a wide range of challenges effectively.
3. **Proven leadership qualities.** I select members who have demonstrated strong leadership qualities in their previous roles. This includes the ability to inspire and motivate others, make difficult decisions, and manage conflicts adeptly. Proven leaders bring stability and confidence to the team.
4. **Commitment to professional growth.** I choose individuals who are committed to continuous professional development. Leaders who prioritise learning and growth are more likely to adapt to changes and drive the school's developmental initiatives forward.
5. **Interpersonal and communication skills.** I ensure that team members possess excellent interpersonal and communication skills. Effective communication is critical for leadership, as it ensures that ideas and values are conveyed clearly, and feedback is constructively given and received. Good interpersonal skills foster a positive working environment and enhance collaboration.

By focusing on these key attributes, I can build a leadership team that is well-equipped to guide the school towards achieving its strategic goals and creating a supportive educational environment.

2.3 Legal and regulatory considerations in recruitment

An essential aspect of effective recruitment in schools involves a thorough understanding of the relevant industrial instruments and awards. These legal frameworks vary significantly across different categories of school staff, such as early learning centre (ELC) personnel, administrative workers, teachers, and casual employees, each governed by distinct conditions and standards.

Knowledge of these regulations is crucial not only for ensuring compliance but also for facilitating fair and transparent hiring practices. By being well-versed in the specific awards applicable to each role, school principals can avoid potential legal pitfalls and ensure that contracts reflect the rights and responsibilities of both the school and its employees accurately. This diligence helps in creating a trustworthy environment where all staff members feel valued and legally protected, thus enhancing the overall recruitment process and ensuring that the school attracts and retains the best possible talent.

When I was deeply involved in the recruitment process, the job description often served as the initial touchpoint between our organisation and potential candidates. It was a critical tool for attracting the right talent, transcending a mere list of duties and requirements to reflect our organisation's culture, values, and vision. Let me share how I guided my team through crafting effective job descriptions that resonated with our ideal candidates:

- **Start with a clear job title.** I insisted that the job title be concise, clear, and free from internal jargon. It needed to accurately reflect the nature of the job and the level of responsibility. I remember chuckling at the transition from "HR Manager" to "Head of People and Culture" – what's in a title, indeed a lot!
- **Provide a concise overview.** We began with a brief overview of the role, giving potential applicants a snapshot of what the job entailed and how it would fit within the larger framework of the organisation. This section was engaging and informative, setting the tone for the rest of the description. It was crucial to have a clear role purpose that everyone on the team could articulate as they promoted the position among colleagues.
- **Detail the core responsibilities.** We listed the primary responsibilities of the role in a clear, bulleted format. It was important to be specific about what the job would entail on a day-to-day basis. This helped candidates assess whether their skills and interests aligned with the job.
- **Specify the required qualifications.** We clearly outlined the necessary qualifications, including education, experience, and technical skills. We were realistic and specific about these requirements to attract qualified candidates, but also aspirational – for instance, if we wanted candidates with a master's degree, we stated it explicitly.
- **Highlight desired skills and competencies.** Beyond the basic qualifications, we mentioned skills and competencies that would make a candidate stand out, such as communication, problem-solving, or leadership qualities. We asked candidates to demonstrate how they exhibited these skills in their daily work.
- **Reflect our school's culture.** The job description gave candidates a sense of our school's culture. We used language that reflected our

values and ethos, attracting candidates who were not only capable but also a good cultural fit. This presupposed our ability to articulate our school's culture succinctly. If we couldn't, we knew we had more work to do.

- **Offer an overview of benefits and perks.** Post-Covid, employees' priorities shifted dramatically, with an increased desire for work–life balance, flexibility, and other non-monetary perks. The pandemic altered the employment landscape, making recruitment challenging and compelling us to offer more than just salaries to attract and retain top talent. Schools with comprehensive benefits packages were more likely to secure skilled and committed employees.

- **Offer a one-year contract.** In educational leadership, offering fixed one-year contracts for new positions was a nuanced decision. While these contracts provided a valuable probationary period to assess the performance of new hires without long-term commitments, they also carried the risk of deterring highly qualified candidates who sought more security. Deciding on fixed-term contracts needed to be strategically tailored to each hiring scenario, balancing the need to attract the best talent with flexibility in staffing decisions. This approach allowed both the school and the staff member to evaluate the fit before making a more permanent commitment, aligning with our goals and maintaining flexibility in our staffing decisions.

- **Include a call to action.** End your job description with a clear call to action. Direct candidates on how to apply and what the next steps will be. Here is one I used for a deputy position I was recruiting for in one of my schools.

> ***Take the next step in your educational leadership journey***
>
> *Are you ready to make a meaningful impact in the world of education? We want to hear from you if you possess a passion for nurturing young minds, a commitment to academic excellence, and a drive for school-wide improvement. As our Deputy Principal, you will play a pivotal role in shaping our educational landscape, inspiring staff and students to achieve their best.*
>
> *Join us in this rewarding journey where your vision and leadership can truly make a difference. Apply now to join our dynamic team and contribute to a legacy of educational excellence. Your skills, experience, and enthusiasm are exactly*

> *what our school needs to continue building a brighter future for all our students.*
>
> *Submit your application today and embark on a fulfilling career that challenges you and offers immense satisfaction in shaping the leaders of tomorrow.*

- **Review and revise.** Finally, review your job description for clarity, tone, and relevance. It is advisable to update the description regularly to reflect any changes in the role or school policy.

By following these guidelines, you can craft job descriptions that capture the spirit of the role and attract the right candidates, making the recruitment process more efficient and effective. Remember, if you invest all the time and energy that you need to in order to have an exemplary recruitment process, you will get the best talent in the market.

2.4 Innovative recruitment strategies

The challenge of attracting and retaining top talent for schools remains a priority. Innovative recruitment strategies have become essential, blending traditional methods with less-conventional solutions to create a dynamic approach to hiring in schools.

Picture a school at the forefront of recruitment innovation. We were the first school in Australia to use a short video clip as part of our recruitment collateral. I leveraged the power of social media to reach potential candidates, utilising platforms like LinkedIn, Twitter (now X), and Instagram, which buzz with activity. Our online presence was not just about showcasing the culture and achievements of our school but also about engaging directly with prospective applicants. I spoke directly, as their would-be boss, to candidates wanting to come and work at our school. They heard from me personally. The video clip brought me into their world. The results were extraordinary.

We built on the first video clip by creating a dynamic and direct line of communication through engaging posts, interactive stories, live Q&A sessions, and groundbreaking short video clips. This approach drew candidates into our vibrant community and provided them with a unique and immersive insight into the open roles at our school.

Imagine the dynamic synergy that we fostered through strategic partnerships with universities and teacher training colleges, exemplified by our close collaboration with the dean of education at our local university, who was on speed dial to assist in placing their finest graduate teachers in our school. These alliances served as a fertile breeding ground for nurturing future educators. Through initiatives like internships, guest lectures by distinguished academics, and collaborative curriculum development, we offered valuable practical experience to emerging teaching professionals and positioned our school at the forefront of talent identification and development. Our school was chosen for a full day immersion for master's students in their final term. This proactive engagement with the academic community enriched our teaching environment and ensured that we were continually invigorated by the latest educational insights and the brightest new educators.

Envision the power of employee referral programs in the context of educational institutions. Current staff members, who already embody the school's values and understand its culture intimately, become invaluable ambassadors in the recruitment process. Through these programs, employees are encouraged to leverage their personal and professional networks to recommend candidates for open positions at the school. These networks often unfold as rich sources of potential candidates, pre-vetted by those who understand what makes someone a good fit for the school's environment. Consequently, referred candidates tend to integrate more seamlessly into the existing team, as they are likely to align closely with the school's ethos and operational dynamics.

This not only speeds up the integration process but also enhances team cohesion and maintains the integrity of the school culture. Furthermore, leveraging employee referrals can lead to higher retention rates and more engaged employees, making it a strategic advantage in building a committed and effective staff.

Data-driven recruitment strategies played a crucial role. By analysing the traits of successful employees, our school tailored its recruitment efforts, fine-tuning job advertisements and selection processes. This analytical approach ensured that each new hire was qualified and a perfect fit for our school's unique environment. This is becoming even more impactful with the use of capabilities and competency frameworks. Our values were a beacon of promise and we delivered.

Our brand story was another critical element. Through our website, social media presence, and active participation in educational forums, we crafted a narrative that resonated with potential candidates. We gave them a compelling case that we were an exceptional employer. The narrative highlighted our values, commitment to success, and the satisfaction of our employees, thereby attracting individuals who share these ideals. From the first post for a job, we were making a case that we were a wonderful school to work at.

Engaging recruitment content – videos, blogs, testimonials – offers a window into life at your school. These narratives provide a realistic view of the work environment and expectations, drawing in candidates who resonate with your school's ethos.

Finally, we would tap into our alumni network. This pool of former students, already instilled with the school's values, was a valuable resource. They returned as potential employees and referred qualified candidates from their professional circles.

In this narrative of innovative recruitment in the education sector, the school emerged as a place of employment and as a dynamic community that nurtures and attracts the best in the field. By integrating traditional methods with creative, modern approaches, it stands at the forefront of educational excellence and has a team of exceptional professionals.

2.5 The art of the interview

Section 1: Tips and techniques for you as the interviewer

Interviewing is an art form, a delicate balance of inquiry and conversation that, when done correctly, can unveil a candidate's true potential. The key lies in asking the right questions and creating an environment where candidates feel comfortable enough to reveal their authentic selves.

I liked asking this question:

> *If we were to ask your team to use three humorous or creative descriptors for your leadership style, what do you think they would say and why?*

Firstly, preparation is paramount. Familiarise yourself thoroughly with the candidate's résumé and the job description. This preparation allows you to tailor your questions, making them relevant and specific. Use open-ended questions to encourage candidates to speak more expansively about their experiences and opinions. For instance, instead of asking, "Did you manage a team?", a more open-ended question would be, "Can you describe your experience in leading and managing teams?"

Active listening is equally crucial. This means hearing their words and paying attention to non-verbal cues. Pauses, eye contact, and body language can often tell you more than their words. It is about understanding the candidate's enthusiasm, hesitation, and confidence, which often lie beneath the surface of their words.

Scenario illustrating active listening

The interviewee, Jordan, is applying for the head of technology role and is discussing the rollout of a new digital transformation project that she was responsible for.

Interviewer: *Thank you for joining us today, Jordan. Can you tell us about the biggest challenge you faced during the digital transformation project at your school?*

Jordan: *Of course. The biggest challenge was definitely managing the resistance to change. Most of the staff were not just hesitant; they were vocal about their doubts. We expected some pushback, but the intensity was surprising. However, once we started showing them tangible benefits, the mood shifted a bit.*

Interviewer: *You mentioned that the intensity of the pushback was surprising. Could you elaborate on what specific aspects of the transformation led to such strong resistance, and how did you address those concerns to eventually shift the mood?*

Jordan: *Well, a lot of the resistance came from our long-term employees who were used to doing things a certain way for years. They were particularly worried about the new software replacing their routine tasks, making them feel obsolete. To address this, we initiated a series of workshops that not only trained them on the new system but also highlighted how these changes would make their daily work more efficient and less tedious. We also created a feedback loop where they could regularly provide input on the system's development, which really helped in making them feel involved in the process.*

Interviewer: *It sounds like involving your employees in the process was key to overcoming their resistance. How do you plan to maintain this level of engagement and address any residual resistance as you continue to implement new technologies?*

This exchange showcases how an interviewer, through active listening, can delve deeper into the underlying causes of a challenge and explore solutions by asking precise and insightful follow-up questions.

Another technique is the use of **situational or behavioural** questions. I liked to ask this question:

> *Imagine you have just implemented a new educational initiative you believe in strongly, but it is met with significant resistance from faculty and parents. How would you navigate this situation to achieve a positive outcome while maintaining the integrity of your initiative and the relationships with those who oppose it?*

Do not ask all interviewees the same questions; customise the interview questions for each candidate depending on their application, experience and suitability. It is wise to have a set of common questions for fairness and for making assessment decisions, but be prepared to be responsive.

These scenarios provide insight into how a candidate has handled situations in the past or how they would handle potential future situations, giving you a glimpse into their practical application of skills and knowledge.

Section 2: Pitfalls and traps to avoid

While mastering the art of interviewing is about utilising effective techniques, it is equally about avoiding common pitfalls that can lead to biased or inaccurate assessments of a candidate.

One major trap is the "halo effect", where an interviewer allows a single positive aspect of the candidate to overshadow all other information. This can lead to an overly favourable evaluation. Be wary of interviewing someone you know very well.

Conversely, the "horn effect" is when a single negative trait affects the interviewer's perception negatively. Both biases can cloud judgment and lead to a decision based more on personal impressions than the candidate's qualifications and potential.

Another common mistake is not providing candidates with enough space to express themselves. Dominating the conversation or interrupting frequently can stifle candidates' ability to fully present their thoughts and experiences. This limits your understanding of the candidate and can create a stressful environment, preventing them from showing their true potential.

There is balance to be struck in interviewing techniques. While it's essential to allow candidates ample space to express themselves, it's equally important to guide the conversation to keep it relevant and concise.

Here's how you might consider addressing a situation where a candidate is excessively verbose or straying off-topic.

- **Use gentle interruptions.** If a candidate begins to stray or their answer becomes too lengthy, use gentle, polite interruptions to steer them back on track. Phrases like "That's really interesting, and I'd like to drill down into one point you made. Could you tell me more about…" This approach helps refocus the discussion without making the candidate feel dismissed.
- **Employ closed questions for clarity.** If a candidate's response is becoming too broad, pivot to using more specific, closed-ended questions that require shorter answers. This can help keep the answers on-topic and concise.
- **Summarise and redirect.** Another effective technique is to summarise what the candidate has said and then lead them to the next topic. For example, "From what you've shared, it sounds like you have extensive experience in project management. Can we now talk about a specific challenge you faced during a project and how you handled it?"

Lastly, avoid asking questions that are too generic. Questions like "What are your strengths?" are so common that most candidates come prepared with rehearsed answers. These do little to reveal the candidate's true character or potential. Tailor your questions to be specific and relevant, challenging the candidate to think and respond genuinely.

A better question to ask is:

> Can you share an instance where your unique skill set made a significant impact on a project or on your team? How did you identify the need, and what was the outcome?

I tried to keep a fairly tight rein on the interview questions and used a script. Not everyone on a panel would stick to the script, which generally was OK, as probing and follow-up questions were important. But I cringed when an interviewer on the panel asked:

> What are your superpowers?

In conclusion, the art of the interview lies in the careful orchestration of questions, active listening, and an awareness of biases. By honing these skills and being mindful of common pitfalls, you can conduct interviews that are insightful, revealing, and instrumental in identifying the best candidates.

2.6 Onboarding for success

Done right, onboarding new staff can lead to a top hire; done wrong, and the new hire may need reworking. The key lies in crafting an onboarding process that imparts necessary information and warmly integrates new staff into the school culture, setting them up for long-term success.

I recall the case of Mr Thompson (the name has been changed), a highly qualified and enthusiastic science teacher who joined our school with great expectations. However, his onboarding experience was a textbook example of what not to do. It was rushed, impersonal, and lacked a structured plan. He received a brief tour of the school, a quick introduction to his colleagues, and was then left to fend for himself. This lack of a structured onboarding process left him feeling isolated and unsupported, struggling to understand the school's culture and expectations. Within months, the school lost a potentially outstanding educator because of this oversight.

This story underscores the importance of a well-thought-out onboarding process. As the principal, I would always make the first call to offer the position to applicants. I loved making the call to someone who was not expecting it. For example, a new graduate was our preferred candidate, and it was evident during the interview, from their humility and modesty, that they did not expect to be offered the job. So when I made the call, they were quite bubbly.

> *Really? Are you serious? This is incredible, I'm genuinely surprised! I wasn't expecting this at all. Thank you so much for this opportunity – I'm truly grateful and excited. You've made my day, if not my entire year. I promise to bring my very best to this role. Thank you again for believing in me and giving me this chance.*

I would also personally ensure that new staff were warmly welcomed into the school community.

Tips for successful onboarding

- **Structured welcome.** The more formal processes I employed usually involved a structured welcome program that included formal introductions to all team members, a copy of the organisational chart, a tour of the school, and an overview of the school's history, mission, values, and future plans.
- **Appropriate training.** Next, it is essential to provide comprehensive training that covers the academic procedures, the school's

administrative systems, communication protocols, and any specific cultural nuances, such as understanding and respecting local customs and traditions, recognising and addressing varying communication styles and social norms, and adapting to the community's educational expectations and values. This interactive training should allow new staff to ask questions and engage with the material actively.
- **Mentorship.** This plays a crucial role in successful onboarding. Pairing new staff with experienced mentors can provide them with ongoing support and guidance. These mentors can help new teachers navigate the school's culture, offer advice on handling classroom challenges, and be a sounding board for new ideas. A recommended structure is provided below.
- **Regular check-ins.** These are also vital, and can be formal meetings or informal catch-ups where new staff can share their experiences, discuss challenges, and receive feedback on their progress. I would routinely check in with all new employees twice in their first year and more frequently as our paths met across the campus.
- **Integration.** Finally, integrating new staff into the school community through social events and professional development activities can help them form connections and feel a part of the team. These are usually reserved for principals and executive leaders, but think about extending them to all new employees, as appropriate.
- **Strategic.** Onboarding should be viewed as a leadership task and an opportunity to lay the foundation for a productive, harmonious, and long-lasting relationship between the new staff and the school. When done correctly, it sets individuals up for success and strengthens the entire educational environment.

An example of a mentorship program timeline for new teacher onboarding

I would like to stick to this framework when onboarding new staff:

> **Week 1.** The new teacher orientation with HR to cover administrative details and introductions to key personnel. Pair new teachers with mentors. First meeting to introduce themselves, discuss roles, and set initial expectations. New teachers shadow their mentors, observing classroom management, teaching methods, and student interactions.

Weeks 2–4. Integration into school culture. Scheduled one-on-one meetings to discuss specific questions, concerns, and experiences. New teachers observe mentors during various classes; mentors observe new teachers and provide feedback. Encourage daily or bi-daily brief check-ins for quick updates or immediate concerns.

Toward the end of the first term. Focus shifts towards refining teaching techniques and managing classroom dynamics. Mentors guide new teachers in identifying and participating in professional development opportunities relevant to their needs.

Second semester. Transition to less-frequent, but more in-depth meetings to discuss long-term goals, challenges, and achievements. New teachers are encouraged to observe and provide feedback to peers, fostering a collaborative environment. Mentors and new teachers collaborate on a small project, like a new curriculum component or school event, to further integrate new teachers into the school community.

End of first year review and future planning. Evaluate the progress of new teachers through discussions with mentors, other faculty, and self-assessments. Based on feedback, new teachers set personal and professional goals for the following year. Organise a small event to celebrate the milestones achieved and the relationships built.

This structured approach ensures that new teachers receive consistent support while gradually taking on more independence, helping them to become confident and effective members of the school community.

Case study – a highly successful innovative onboarding program

One truly innovative and creative onboarding technique that stands out for its effectiveness is the "immersion project". This technique involves assigning a new hire a mini project during their first few weeks. The project is designed to be achievable within a short period and offers a hands-on way for the new employees to immerse themselves in the company culture, workflow, and team dynamics.

Let us consider a practical example that demonstrates its effectiveness in a school setting. The new science teacher, Mr Thompson, joins the faculty at the start of the academic year. For his immersion project, Mr Thompson is assigned to develop a small-scale science fair project that aligns with the curriculum and involves students from different classes.

Project assignment. Mr Thompson is tasked with organising a mini science fair focusing on renewable energy sources. This project is relevant to his role as a science teacher and is designed to be achievable within the first month of his tenure.

Cross-departmental interaction. To successfully complete this project, Mr Thompson collaborates with the school's art department for creative display ideas, the IT department for technical support on presentations, and fellow science teachers for content alignment. This interaction not only helps him build a professional network within the school but also provides a practical understanding of how collaborative projects are managed.

Mentorship and support. An experienced teacher, Mrs Allen, who has previously organised similar events, is assigned as Mr Thompson's mentor. She guides him through the process, from initial planning to execution, providing insights into effective student engagement and project management within the school.

Presentation and feedback. At the completion of the science fair, Mr Thompson presents the outcomes and his learnings to the school's leadership and his department. This presentation allows him to highlight his organisational and teaching skills and receive valuable feedback from peers and superiors.

Reflection and integration. Following the presentation, Mr Thompson engages in a reflection session with Mrs Allen and the principal, discussing what he learned about the school's approach to interdisciplinary projects, student engagement, and the integration of technology in teaching. He also articulates how he can apply these insights to his everyday teaching responsibilities and future projects.

This example of the immersion project illustrates its efficacy in helping new employees quickly adapt to their roles while actively contributing to the school's objectives. By engaging in meaningful work from the outset, Mr Thompson not only gains a deeper understanding of the school's operational and cultural dynamics but also feels a stronger sense of belonging and commitment to his new environment.

2.7 Cultivating a culture of continuous learning

I am including a case study from outside of schools, TechForward, to make visible what cultivating a culture of continuous learning can look like. I like this case study because it draws from a company that is at the cutting edge of one of today's most significant challenges for school leaders, artificial intelligence (AI).

In the heart of Silicon Valley, nestled within the bustling streets and innovative spirit, stood TechForward, a company renowned for its cutting-edge technology and dynamic workforce. The CEO, Elizabeth Chen, believed fervently in the power of continuous learning. She was particularly fascinated by the potential of artificial intelligence.

Under her leadership, TechForward embarked on integrating AI-driven analytics to predict market trends, enabling the company to not only respond to customer needs with unprecedented speed but also to anticipate changes before they occurred. She knew that to stay ahead in the rapidly evolving tech industry, her team needed not just to adapt but to thrive in an environment of perpetual growth and learning, harnessing groundbreaking technologies like AI to drive innovation and maintain a competitive edge.

As Elizabeth walked through the open-plan office, she observed her team engaged in various activities. Some were huddled around a whiteboard, brainstorming solutions; others were deep in concentration, coding; and a few were in a workshop, learning about the latest advancements in artificial intelligence. This was the culture she had dreamt of creating – a place where learning was not just encouraged but ingrained in the very fabric of the company.

Embracing a learning mindset

Elizabeth knew that cultivating a culture of continuous learning started with mindset. She often held town hall meetings, sharing stories of innovation and perseverance, emphasising the importance of a growth mindset. "Every challenge," she would say, "is an opportunity to learn and grow."

Learning in the flow of work

TechForward had seamlessly integrated learning into the daily workflow. Project debriefs included learning sessions, where successes and failures were dissected for lessons. Regular "learning lunches" were organised, where team members shared knowledge and skills with their colleagues, fostering a sense of community and collaborative learning.

Personalised learning paths

Understanding that each employee had unique learning needs and styles, Elizabeth had invested in a platform that offered personalised learning paths. Employees could choose courses relevant to their interests and career goals, making learning more engaging and effective.

Encouraging experimentation and accepting failure

At TechForward, experimentation was celebrated, and failure was viewed as a stepping stone to success. Elizabeth had created an "Innovation Lab" where employees could work on passion projects, experiment with new ideas, and learn from their attempts, regardless of the outcome.

Recognising and rewarding learning

To keep the learning momentum, Elizabeth ensured that continuous learning was recognised and rewarded. Employees who demonstrated a commitment to personal and professional growth were celebrated in monthly meetings, inspiring others to follow suit.

As Elizabeth reflected on the learning culture at TechForward, she felt a sense of pride. She had fostered an environment where learning was a continuous journey, where each day brought new opportunities for growth. In this dynamic landscape of technology, she knew that the continuous learning culture at TechForward was not just a strategy, but a necessity for thriving in an ever-evolving world.

In reviewing the case of TechForward and the visionary approach of CEO Elizabeth Chen, we see a vivid illustration of what cultivating a culture of continuous learning can truly look like. The narrative of TechForward is more than a success story; it is a blueprint for fostering an environment where learning, innovation, and growth are not just sporadic events but a continuous journey.

Note: TechForward is a fictional company created for illustrative purposes.

Now, as the reader and a leader in your own right, I challenge you to take inspiration from this case study and apply it within your own context. Here is your challenge:

Design a 3-year action plan for cultivating a culture of continuous learning in your workplace

Throughout this three-year journey, remember that the goal is to create an environment akin to what Elizabeth achieved at TechForward – a place where learning is as natural as breathing, where each day is an opportunity to grow, and where the pursuit of knowledge is interwoven into the very fabric of your organisation.

The journey of continuous learning is ongoing and ever-evolving. As you embark on this challenge, keep in mind that the true measure of success will be the extent to which learning becomes an integral part of your organisation's DNA. It is not just about the programs you implement, but the learning culture you cultivate. Let your action plan be the first step in this transformative journey.

2.8 Professional development (PD) programs

When it came to nurturing a successful educational environment, I quickly learned the critical role of well-structured PD programs. These programs were pivotal in enhancing teacher capabilities, which, in turn, directly impacted student learning outcomes. To ensure I developed top-shelf PD programs for teachers and middle leaders, I adhered to 10 foundational principles:

1. **Relevance and customisation.** I tailored the PD programs to meet the specific needs of the teachers and leaders they were designed for. They addressed current educational trends, technological advances, and specific challenges faced in the classroom. As technology advanced and global connectivity increased, customising content became even more essential.
2. **Collaborative learning.** I encouraged collaborative learning environments where educators could share experiences, strategies, and insights. This approach fostered a sense of community and collective growth.
3. **Continuous and sustained learning.** I viewed effective PD not as a one-off event but as a continuous process. My programs offered ongoing support and resources, allowing educators to continually develop their skills.
4. **Active learning.** The PD programs involved teachers in hands-on activities, not just lectures. This active participation enhanced learning and retention.
5. **Feedback and reflection.** I incorporated mechanisms for feedback and self-reflection, enabling educators to evaluate their progress and identify areas for improvement.
6. **Expert facilitation.** The facilitators of our PD programs were experts in their fields, capable of inspiring and engaging educators. Their expertise was crucial in delivering content that was both credible and compelling. It was essential that facilitators had contextual leadership

experience in a school setting and had the time and resources to commit to the PD programs beyond one-off events.

7. **Practical application.** While theoretical knowledge was essential, I ensured the PD programs also focused on the practical application of these concepts in classroom settings.
8. **Use of technology.** I leveraged technology to make learning more interactive and accessible, including using online platforms for resources, discussions, and virtual workshops.
9. **Recognition and incentives.** I recognised and rewarded participation and achievements in PD programs. This could be in the form of certificates, credits, or acknowledgments that motivated educators to engage actively.
10. **Evaluation and iteration.** I regularly evaluated the effectiveness of PD programs and was willing to make iterative changes. This ensured that the programs remained relevant and impactful.

Implementing these principles transformed mundane PD programs into dynamic and impactful learning experiences. It created an environment where educators were not just passive recipients of information, but active participants in a journey of continuous professional growth. In this way, professional development transcended the traditional boundaries of training, becoming a cornerstone in the lifelong journey of educational excellence.

However, to avoid pitfalls in designing PD programs, there were several things I steered clear of:

- **One-size-fits-all approach.** I avoided generic PD programs that did not consider teachers' varying skill levels, subject areas, and interests. Tailoring content to address diverse needs and providing options for different learning paths prevented frustration.
- **Lack of practical relevance.** Teachers often became disenchanted with PD programs heavy on theory but light on practical application. They needed strategies and skills that they could immediately apply in their classrooms. I ensured that PD felt connected to the realities of everyday teaching.
- **Ignoring teacher feedback and input.** I never ignored teacher feedback or excluded their input in the planning process. Teachers were more likely to appreciate and engage with PD when they felt their experiences and insights were valued and reflected in the program.

By adhering to these guidelines and avoiding these pitfalls, the PD programs I created were more effective, engaging, and valued by teachers, leading to a more positive impact on their teaching practice and overall school culture.

2.9 Mentoring and coaching

In the discourse of staff development within education, consultants like to differentiate between "mentoring" and "coaching", each serving distinct but complementary functions in my opinion.

Mentoring typically involves a longer-term relationship focused on the holistic development of the mentee, drawing on the personal experiences and wisdom of the mentor. It is often characterised by a broader scope, aiming to nurture the mentee's overall career and personal growth.

Coaching, particularly instructional coaching as outlined by resources like AITSL (2024), tends to be more focused and structured. It involves specific goals and skills development, such as classroom management techniques, instructional strategies, and integrating technology effectively in teaching. Instructional coaching is intensely practical and often short-term, aimed at enhancing immediate teaching practices rather than the broader career trajectory.

Both roles are invaluable; however, the key to their effectiveness lies in their appropriate application. While coaching might address immediate instructional challenges, mentoring can help develop a reflective practitioner over time, shaping educators who are not only skilled in the classroom but also wise and adaptive in their broader professional lives.

I liken the impact of mentoring and coaching to the influential role of a skilled sports coach. Drawing parallels with Wayne Bennett (2009), one of Australia's greatest rugby league coaches, is particularly illustrative in this context. Bennett's coaching career, marked by an extraordinary ability to build and guide successful teams, mirrors the essential qualities of effective educational mentoring and coaching.

Bennett's approach to coaching was never solely about the technicalities of rugby league; it was about cultivating a team culture, nurturing individual player strengths, and steering them toward a unified vision of success. This philosophy aligns seamlessly with the role of mentors and coaches in an educational setting. They are not just disseminators of knowledge but catalysts for personal and professional growth. They guide educators through the complex landscape of teaching, just as Bennett navigated the intricacies of rugby league.

Implementing a successful mentoring and coaching program in education requires a few Bennett-esque strategies. The first is effective pairing. Like assembling a winning rugby league team, mentor-mentee matching should be based on complementary strengths, shared interests, and targeted growth areas.

Regular, structured interactions are vital. These should resemble the team meetings in rugby league, where strategies are devised, performance is reviewed, and feedback is exchanged openly. Setting clear, attainable goals in these interactions is key – much like the tactical objectives in a rugby league match.

Like a successful rugby league team, the foundation of the mentor-mentee relationship must be trust and confidentiality. The bond of mutual respect and trust is what allows for genuine growth and open communication.

Another page from Bennett's playbook is the encouragement of reflective practice. This might involve analysing match footage to critique and improve performance in sports. It translates to reflecting on teaching methodologies, classroom management, and professional challenges in education.

Upskilling in schools, when approached with a coaching philosophy akin to that of renowned sports coach Wayne Bennett, transforms professional development into a strategic and nurturing process.

By adopting the role of a coach, educational leaders can effectively identify and enhance the unique strengths and potential of each educator. This approach not only sharpens the individual skills of educators but also fosters an environment of mutual respect, collaboration, and shared vision – elements that are essential for a successful sports team. Such an environment encourages educators to reflect on their practices, embrace continuous learning, and develop resilience, thereby cultivating a culture of excellence and continuous improvement. Ultimately, this methodology mirrors the successful strategies used in sports coaching, focusing on building cohesive and supportive relationships that drive team performance and success.

This coaching mindset has allowed me to focus not just on the immediate educational goals but on the larger picture of personal and professional growth. It has been about inspiring confidence, instilling a sense of purpose, and guiding educators through challenges and triumphs alike.

The satisfaction of seeing a team member overcome a hurdle or grow in confidence and skill echoes the pride a sports coach feels in witnessing the development and success of their players.

In every interaction, workshop, or meeting, I have embodied this core philosophy – the conviction that a good coach can alter the course of a game, but a great coach can transform a life. This principle has served as the bedrock of my methodology in mentoring and coaching within the educational sphere. It represents my contribution to the intricate network of teaching and learning, intertwining elements of guidance, support, and ongoing education to forge a robust and enduring framework.

As educators, we are all coaches in our own right. We shape minds, guide journeys, and influence futures. Embracing this role with intention and passion, as I have tried to do, can turn the act of coaching from a mere role into an impactful, lasting legacy.

An effective mentoring relationship, integral to this philosophy, consists of several key components:

- **Trust and confidentiality**, which serve as the foundation, allowing for open and honest communication
- **Mutual respect and empathy**, which foster a safe and supportive environment conducive to learning and growth
- **Goal setting**, which aligns the mentor and mentee towards specific professional aspirations and educational outcomes
- **Feedback and reflection**, which are crucial for continuous improvement and personal development
- **Commitment and accountability**, which ensure both parties are engaged and responsible for the mentoring process.

These elements work synergistically to create a dynamic and enriching experience that not only enhances the professional capabilities of the educators but also deeply impacts their personal growth and the educational outcomes of the students they serve.

2.10 Performance evaluation and feedback

In schools, performance evaluation and feedback are pivotal in fostering growth and development. The effectiveness of these systems can significantly impact the morale, motivation, and professional progression of educators. Some leaders run from the concept "performance evaluation", but I advocate it is essential in high-performing schools.

To illustrate the stark contrast between highly effective and poor, ineffective systems, I want to share with readers a table that I developed to make visible the difference. This is a framework that I used effectively.

Aspect	Highly effective performance evaluation systems	Poor, ineffective systems of feedback
Objective setting	Goals are collaboratively set, aligning with both the individual's aspirations and the institution's objectives.	Goals are often unilaterally imposed, misaligned with personal career goals or the school's vision.
Regular check-ins	Frequent and scheduled check-ins ensure ongoing support and timely feedback.	Sporadic or non-existent check-ins lead to a lack of guidance and support.
Comprehensive approach	Evaluations cover a range of criteria, including teaching effectiveness, student engagement, professional development, and contribution to the school community.	Evaluations focus narrowly, often only on test scores or administrative compliance.
Feedback quality	Constructive and specific feedback that highlights areas of success and opportunities for growth.	Vague or generic feedback, often focused only on negatives without actionable advice.
Professional growth	Emphasis on professional development with clear pathways for improvement and advancement.	Lack of focus on professional growth or development opportunities.
Communication style	Open and honest communication, encouraging dialogue and understanding.	One-way communication, with little opportunity for the educator to voice opinions or concerns.

Aspect	Highly effective performance evaluation systems	Poor, ineffective systems of feedback
Cultural sensitivity	Acknowledges and respects diverse teaching styles and cultural backgrounds.	Overlooks cultural and individual diversity, imposing a one-size-fits-all standard.
Use of data	Data is used as one of multiple tools to assess performance, not the sole basis.	Over-reliance on quantitative data, ignoring qualitative aspects of teaching.
Follow-up	Follow-up meetings are scheduled to review progress on feedback and goals.	No follow-up, leaving educators unsure about the impact of the evaluation.
Recognition and rewards	Performance achievements are recognised and rewarded, fostering motivation.	Little to no recognition for good performance, leading to diminished morale.

This table encapsulates the core features of effective performance evaluation and feedback systems versus those that fail to meet the mark. By understanding and implementing effective performance evaluation systems, schools can create a more supportive, growth-oriented, and fair environment for their staff, ultimately leading to enhanced educational outcomes.

2.11 Retention strategies

Retaining top talent in schools, particularly within the heavily unionised context of Australia, presents unique challenges. The traditional lever of monetary incentives, such as bonuses and above-award payments, is often not feasible due to the standardised nature of pay scales and union agreements. This limitation necessitates a more intrinsic approach to staff retention, especially now that the workforce often seeks more than just financial rewards from their jobs.

In this era, educators, like many professionals, are increasingly driven by factors beyond the pay check. They seek fulfilment, recognition, and a sense of belonging. Thus, schools must adopt innovative strategies to retain their top talent, focusing on creating an environment that nurtures and values its staff.

- **Professional development and career growth.** One of the key strategies is to invest in professional development and career growth opportunities. Teachers are lifelong learners by nature, and providing avenues for them to enhance their skills and take on new challenges can be a powerful motivator. This includes offering ongoing training, support for further education, and opportunities for career advancement within the school.
- **Supportive leadership and school culture.** The role of leadership in creating a positive and supportive school culture cannot be overstated. A leadership style that is inclusive, values feedback, and recognises the contributions of staff can significantly enhance job satisfaction and loyalty. Creating a culture where teachers feel valued, heard, and part of a larger mission can foster a deep sense of commitment.
- **Work-life balance and well-being.** Acknowledging and supporting the work-life balance of educators is critical. This can be addressed through flexible working arrangements, providing support for mental and physical health, and ensuring a sustainable workload. A school that cares for the well-being of its staff not only boosts morale but also reduces burnout and turnover.
- **Community and connection.** Building a strong sense of community within the school can also enhance retention. This involves fostering relationships and connections among staff through team-building activities, social events, and collaborative projects. When teachers feel connected to their colleagues and their school, their job satisfaction increases.
- **Recognition and appreciation.** Regular and genuine recognition of staff achievements and contributions can also be a powerful retention tool. This recognition doesn't have to be monetary; it can be as simple as acknowledging a job well done in staff meetings, celebrating professional milestones, or providing positive feedback for effective teaching practices.
- **Clear remuneration pathways.** Along with transparent earning opportunities, these have also become huge for Gen Xers.

While the challenges of staff retention in Australian schools are compounded by the inability to use monetary incentives significantly, there are numerous other strategies that can be employed. By focusing on intrinsic motivators such as professional growth, supportive leadership, work-life balance, community, and recognition, schools can create an environment where top talent not only chooses to stay but is also motivated to thrive.

While traditional monetary incentives may be limited due to regulatory and budgetary constraints, there are significant non-monetary benefits that can be equally, if not more, motivating. An effective strategy is the provision of support for further education – covering costs for advanced degrees such as master's or PhDs. This approach not only offers a substantial incentive to educational professionals but also enriches the intellectual capital within the school.

By investing in the continued professional development of staff through scholarships or funding for higher education, schools can foster a culture of lifelong learning and innovation. Such incentives not only enhance the appeal of staying long-term within the institution but also ensure that the school benefits from the advanced knowledge and fresh perspectives that further-educated teachers bring back to their classrooms and the broader school community.

In my own leadership experience, I have always placed a high value on generosity, particularly when it comes to granting leave. Understanding the intense demands placed on educators, I believed in offering more flexible and generous leave options than what the awards typically stipulated. This approach was not just about giving time off; it was a tangible expression of trust and care towards my staff.

This generosity in granting leave was one of my key strategies in staff retention. It demonstrated a deep respect for the personal lives and well-being of my team members. This approach fostered a culture of mutual respect and appreciation, contributing significantly to high morale and loyalty among the staff. Educators knew that their well-being was a priority, and this understanding translated into a deeper commitment to their roles and the school. In turn, this approach helped in creating a more vibrant, positive, and productive educational environment.

2.12 Broader philosophical implications of leadership development

Leadership is not merely a role occupied or a list of achievements completed; it is deeply intertwined with personal growth and the understanding of one's core identity.

Embracing the Socratic maxim that "An unexamined life is not worth living", it becomes evident that truly effective leaders are those who understand the origins and evolution of their leadership journey. This introspection isn't just about self-awareness but is also about recognising the virtues that underpin one's approach to leadership.

Leaders come to their roles through various paths:

- **Being.** Some leaders perceive their identity as inherently tied to leadership, feeling a natural alignment with leading others from an early age.
- **Engaging.** Others step into leadership roles through the act of engaging with and mobilising people towards common goals, especially in response to immediate challenges.
- **Performing.** There are those whose leadership is closely linked to their career progression, viewing each position held as a step in their leadership development.
- **Accepting.** And some recognise their leadership only upon seeing their influence on others, understanding their impact through the respect and followship they garner (Roberts, 2024).

Beyond these pathways, it is crucial to distinguish between "résumé virtues" – skills one learns for career advancement – and "eulogy virtues", which speak to one's character and the deeper legacy one leaves behind. Inspired by David Brooks' exploration of these concepts, it is essential for leaders, especially those at the helm of educational institutions, to cultivate virtues like humility, compassion, and kindness. These qualities often transcend the professional realm and define a leader's true value to their community and society at large.

Leadership shapes and is shaped by these deeper virtues, fostering a transformation that is profound. It is not only about maturity; it is about becoming a person of influence and integrity, someone who inspires and enacts positive change. In this light, every leader should reflect not just on how they lead but on who they become through their leadership journey. This reflective practice not only enhances their effectiveness but also ensures they leave a legacy that aligns with the most cherished values of humanity (Roberts, 2024).

2.13 Key takeaways

In this chapter, we've explored various aspects of educational leadership, each crucial to achieving our schools' ultimate aim of nurturing excellence. As we dissected these facets, I've gathered some essential insights that I believe are instrumental for anyone stepping into a leadership role within education. Let me share these key takeaways with you:

1. **The art of the interview.** Always aim to ask insightful questions that cut through the surface and reveal a candidate's true potential. Steer clear of those generic questions that everyone prepares for. Instead, probe deeper to uncover how a candidate truly thinks and reacts in diverse situations.

2. **Onboarding for success.** It's crucial to establish effective onboarding practices that smoothly integrate new staff into your school culture. Make them feel valued and well-prepared from day one. Remember, a successful onboarding process can significantly influence a new staff member's ability to thrive and connect with both colleagues and students.

3. **Cultivating a culture of continuous learning.** Emphasise the need to foster an environment of continuous learning and development, much like the dynamics observed in successful sports teams. This approach not only enhances skills but also builds a resilient and adaptive team.

4. **Performance evaluation and feedback.** Lay out clear, fair, and constructive principles for performance evaluations. Contrast what makes an evaluation system effective versus what can render it ineffective. Remember, the goal of performance evaluation should always be to inspire growth, not to induce fear.

5. **Retention strategies.** Discuss the power of non-monetary strategies for staff retention. Focus on intrinsic motivators such as professional development opportunities, work–life balance, and a supportive school culture. These elements often hold more weight than financial incentives in nurturing long-term commitment and satisfaction.

By embracing these principles, you're not just managing a school; you're leading a community toward greater achievement and satisfaction. Remember, the strength of your leadership is measured not by the obedience it commands, but by the empowerment it imparts.

My approach to educational leadership reflects a philosophy that blends strategic planning with empathy, flexibility, and a deep commitment to staff development and well-being.

The journey of an educational leader is one of constant learning and adaptation, and it is my hope that the insights shared in this chapter will serve as valuable signposts for current and aspiring leaders in the educational realm.

The goal is not just to lead but to inspire, not just to manage but to empower, and not just to educate but to transform. When addressing an underperforming member of staff, it is crucial to approach the conversation with a blend of honesty and support. Start by clearly outlining the observed performance issues and then engage in a constructive dialogue, focusing on understanding their challenges and exploring potential solutions together. This approach fosters a supportive atmosphere that encourages improvement while maintaining respect and dignity.

CHAPTER 3

THE CULTURE CONUNDRUM
*Shaping and sustaining
school culture*

It would be great to do a study on what all schools agree upon regarding "great" school culture and how it is achieved and sustained. Perhaps this is a thesis for a leader contemplating a PhD or EdD.

3.1 Understanding school culture

Culture often trumps strategy, but a poor culture can severely disrupt a well-laid strategy. In the complexity of a school environment, the often overlooked yet pivotal element that unites every facet is the school culture. It is an amalgam of values, beliefs, traditions, and behaviours that shape the daily experiences of students, teachers, and staff. For principals, understanding this culture is not merely a leadership task; it is akin to a gardener understanding the soil and climate before planting. It involves discerning the nuances that make each school unique.

School culture is the heartbeat of a school, pulsating through the hallways and classrooms. It influences how students learn, how teachers teach, and how the community interacts. A positive culture fosters an environment where students feel safe and valued, teachers feel respected and motivated, and learning thrives. Conversely, a negative culture can stifle innovation, hinder academic achievement, and lead to a disengaged community.

Arguably, an organisation with international recognition for its strong culture, where the brand is a reflection of this culture, is Google (now part of Alphabet Inc.). Google's corporate culture (Panmore Institute, 2023) is renowned for its emphasis on innovation, creativity, and inclusiveness, which aligns seamlessly with its brand identity as a leading technology company.

Key aspects of Google's culture include:

- **Innovation and creativity.** Google encourages a culture of experimentation and risk-taking, which has led to the development of groundbreaking products and services. This culture of innovation is a core part of their brand identity.
- **Open and collaborative environment.** The company is known for its open workspaces and collaborative approach, fostering community and teamwork. This is reflected in how Google products often emphasise user collaboration and sharing.
- **Employee well-being and benefits.** Google is famous for its employee perks, such as gourmet cafeterias, wellness centres, and on-site childcare. These benefits reflect the company's commitment to the well-being of its employees, which, in turn, is mirrored in its brand image as a company that cares.
- **Learning and development.** Continuous learning and development are ingrained in Google's culture. The company offers various resources for employee education and skill development, aligning with its brand as an innovator and leader in technology.
- **Diversity and inclusion.** Google strongly emphasises diversity and inclusion, which are cultural elements and brand characteristics. The company's efforts to create inclusive products and services further reinforce this aspect of its culture and brand.

Overall, Google's strong culture is a critical driver of its success and a defining element of its brand, which is recognised and admired worldwide. This synergy between culture and brand is a key reason why Google continues to attract top talent and maintain its position as a leader in the tech industry.

As a principal, assessing and understanding a school's current cultural landscape begins with keen observation and active listening. Walk the halls, visit classrooms, and attend school events. Observe the interactions between students, staff, and parents. Listen not just to what is being said but also to what is not being said. Is there a sense of enthusiasm and engagement, or do you detect undertones of stress and apathy?

Engaging in conversations with a cross-section of the school community is invaluable. Speak with teachers, students, support staff, and parents to gather diverse perspectives. Speak with the cleaning contractor or cleaners; they know! Ask open-ended questions about their experiences and perceptions of the school. This dialogue can reveal insights into the strengths of the school's culture and areas that may need attention.

I would ask these questions:

1. Can you describe a typical day at our school?
2. What aspects do you find most enjoyable, and which are challenging?
3. How do you feel about how communication happens here between different groups (such as teachers, students, support staff, and parents)?
4. What examples can you give of effective or ineffective communication?
5. What do you think are the key values of our school?
6. How do you see these values being reflected in the school's activities and decisions?

Surveys and focus groups are also effective tools in gauging school culture. They can provide quantitative and qualitative data that offers a broader view of the school's climate. Analyse this data not just for trends and patterns but for the stories it tells about the lived experiences of the school community.

Remember, the goal of understanding school culture is not to judge or critique but to empathise and comprehend. It is about building a foundation of knowledge upon which strategies to enhance the culture can be developed. As a principal, your role is to be both a custodian and a cultivator of the school's culture, nurturing it to ensure every member of the school community can flourish.

Understanding school culture is a journey that requires curiosity, empathy, and a commitment to continuous improvement. It's a journey well worth taking, for the culture of a school is not just about the here and now; it shapes the future of every individual who walks through its doors.

3.2 Culture trumps strategy (Merchant, 2011)

In educational leadership, the importance of strategy is often heralded as the key to successful school management and improvement. However, I suggest that a strong and positive school culture holds more sway in determining the success of any strategic plan.

An exemplar of educational leadership driving societal change can be seen in our initiative to embrace inclusive education practices long before they became a societal norm. By fostering an environment that valued diversity and inclusion from the early stages, we not only improved educational outcomes for underrepresented groups but also influenced broader societal attitudes towards diversity. This case study illustrates how schools can indeed lead the way in societal transformation, becoming navigators of change rather than mere responders to external pressures.

This subchapter examines the intricate relationship between school culture and strategy, arguing that even the most meticulously crafted strategies can falter without a supportive and aligned cultural environment.

Understanding the interplay between culture and strategy

The symbiotic relationship between school culture and strategy is at the heart of this discussion. School culture, the collective norms, values, beliefs, and behaviours within a school community, is the bedrock upon which strategies are built and implemented. Culture can either bolster or undermine strategic plans, emphasising the need for alignment between the two for successful implementation.

I like to look beyond schools to make concepts visible to our readers. A compelling example of how simple practices can reinforce powerful cultural values is seen in the All Blacks rugby team's tradition of cleaning their own dressing room after matches. This ritual underscores the principles that no individual is above the team, and that humility and accountability are as important as any skill on the field.

Emulating such practices in a school setting, where staff and students alike participate in maintaining their environments, can foster a culture of mutual respect and collective responsibility. These small actions are symbolic but powerful, reinforcing a culture where pride and humility triumph over ego, aligning perfectly with the ethos of educational institutions where developing character is as crucial as academic achievement.

Describing the culture of the All Blacks (Kerr, 2013), the renowned New Zealand rugby team, in just three words is challenging given the depth and complexity of their ethos. However, focusing on these three key elements makes the connection between culture and strategy.

1. **Excellence.** The All Blacks are known for their relentless pursuit of high performance and excellence, both on and off the field.

2. **Teamwork.** They emphasise a strong sense of unity and collaboration, where the team's success is placed above individual achievements.
3. **Respect.** This encompasses respect for the game, respect for opponents, respect for their cultural heritage (notably through the haka), and respect for one another within the team.

The ethos of the All Blacks illustrates how deeply culture influences a team's strategic outcomes. These values of excellence, teamwork, and respect not only define their interactions but also guide their strategic decisions and achievements. As we turn our focus from the sports field to the educational arena, it's equally critical to assess how well a school's culture can support and adapt to strategic changes.

Assessing cultural readiness for change

Before embarking on strategic changes, evaluating the current school culture's readiness for these changes is crucial. This assessment involves understanding staff attitudes, existing norms, and the overall emotional climate of the school. The school leader's job is to gauge whether their school is culturally prepared to embrace and support new strategic initiatives. To do this, the school leader could conduct a culture audit.

To conduct a comprehensive culture audit within our school, I focused on gathering deep, actionable insights through a two-pronged approach: one-on-one interviews and a broad survey of all staff members.

I began by conducting one-on-one interviews with a stratified sample of our staff. This involved selecting individuals from various roles and seniority levels to ensure a diverse range of perspectives were captured. These interviews were designed to understand the employees' experiences and perceptions of our school's culture. I asked open-ended questions to encourage detailed responses and listened attentively to understand the nuances of their experiences and viewpoints. This method not only provided me with in-depth qualitative data but also helped in building trust and openness among the staff.

Simultaneously, I deployed a comprehensive survey to all staff members to quantify their perceptions of the workplace culture. The survey included questions about various aspects of our school environment, such as communication, collaboration, respect, and job satisfaction. It was essential to ensure anonymity to allow staff to express their honest opinions without fear of repercussion.

After collecting the data, I meticulously analysed the findings from both the interviews and surveys. This analysis highlighted several key themes and areas needing attention. From there, I synthesised the insights into a report that outlined actionable goals aimed at addressing the specific cultural issues identified. These goals were crafted with the intent to foster a more positive, collaborative, and supportive working environment.

Implementing these changes was a phased process, involving ongoing communication with the staff and regular reassessment to measure progress. By conducting this culture audit, I aimed to ensure that our school's environment aligned more closely with our values and the needs of everyone in our community.

Cultural barriers to strategic implementation

Even the best strategies can face roadblocks if cultural barriers exist. Where, in your school, could the potential cultural obstacles, such as resistance to change, entrenched practices, or misalignment with the school's core values, impede the success of new strategies? How can these barriers be addressed and overcome?

Addressing cultural barriers to strategic implementation requires an understanding of the specific obstacles that can arise in a school environment. Here are some examples of potential cultural obstacles and strategies to overcome them:

- **Resistance to change**

  Example: Teachers and staff may be accustomed to traditional methods of teaching and might resist adopting new educational technologies or innovative teaching strategies.

  Solution: Implement change-management practices that include training and development sessions to ease the transition. Engage teachers in the decision-making process to give them a sense of ownership and control over the changes.

- **Entrenched practices**

  Example: Long-standing administrative processes may be inefficient but persist because they are deeply ingrained in the school's operations.

  Solution: Conduct workshops that demonstrate the benefits of new practices versus old ones. Use pilot projects to showcase the effectiveness of new methods in a controlled, measurable way to build support for wider implementation.

- **Misalignment with school's core values**

    Example: A new policy aimed at increasing academic rigour might inadvertently stress competition over the school's core value of collaborative learning.

    Solution: Realign the policy to include collaborative elements, such as group projects or peer reviews, ensuring that new strategies do not stray from the school's foundational values.

- **Communication gaps**

    Example: Key strategic decisions are made by the school leadership without sufficient input or communication with the teaching staff, leading to misunderstanding and lack of support.

    Solution: Establish regular communication channels, such as town hall meetings or feedback sessions, where strategies can be discussed openly and input can be actively solicited from staff at all levels.

- **Lack of professional development**

    Example: Teachers may feel unprepared to implement new curriculum standards because of insufficient training.

    Solution: Invest in ongoing professional development programs that are specifically tailored to new curricular demands and teaching methodologies, ensuring teachers feel competent and confident in their roles.

By identifying and addressing these cultural barriers head-on, school principals can significantly enhance the successful implementation of new strategies, ensuring that they lead to meaningful improvements rather than becoming another layer of challenge in the school's operations.

Aligning culture with strategic goals

Alignment is key in ensuring that the school culture supports and enhances the strategic goals. Can you develop strategies to align school culture with the intended strategic direction? This includes leadership modelling desired cultural traits, revising cultural norms to support strategic goals, and ensuring that communication around strategic changes reinforces cultural values.

Sustaining culture during strategic change

Change is constant, but maintaining a positive and consistent school culture during these periods is vital. How can you focus on leveraging cultural strengths to support transitions and new initiatives, ensuring that the school's culture remains a steady and supportive force amid strategic change?

In my time as a principal, I found myself at the centre of a cultural whirlwind at a school steeped in a century-old tradition: the mandatory wearing of gloves during winter. This quaint practice, while cherished as a symbol of elegance and discipline by our esteemed alumni, had increasingly become a source of discomfort among our current students.

The requests to drop this glove mandate initially started as a trickle from students and parents, and soon swelled into a deluge. Engaging with these voices was crucial, not only to address their concerns but to foster a sense of inclusivity and responsiveness in our school culture.

Our student leadership team, representing the voice of the student body, played a pivotal role in advocating for this change. They organised forums and surveys to gauge student opinion, presenting a compelling case that the glove tradition, though revered, was impractical and outdated in the modern educational environment. Their involvement was instrumental in demonstrating to the wider community that our students were not just recipients of school culture but active participants in its evolution.

Simultaneously, the staff leadership also showed strong support for reevaluating the tradition. They recognised the importance of adapting to changing times and maintaining relevance in our students' lives. By bridging the gap between the revered traditions of the past and the practical needs of the present, they underscored the school's commitment to progressive leadership.

Deciding to unclasp this tradition sparked a flurry of excitement among the students, who were more than ready to bid farewell to their frosty-fingered woes. However, it ruffled the feathers of our "old girls", who viewed the gloves as a cherished emblem of their own school days.

The great "Glove Debate" turned out to be a humorous yet pivotal moment in our school's history, symbolising the inevitable clash between cherished tradition and practical modernity. It was a light-hearted yet significant reminder that even the smallest elements of school culture can carry profound meaning and impact. This incident underscored the importance of giving voice to all stakeholders in our community, affirming that the path to meaningful change is paved with dialogue, respect, and collaboration.

3.3 The principal's role in culture building

In schools, the role of a principal extends far beyond management duties and curriculum oversight. At the heart of their responsibilities lies a crucial yet often underappreciated task – culture building. This subchapter dissects the myriad ways in which principals can effectively shape and influence school culture, offering actionable strategies to become leaders and role models in this transformative process.

1. **The power of influence** a principal holds over school culture is profound and pervasive. They set the tone for the entire school, and their actions, attitudes, and values are mirrored throughout the institution. However, principals must recognise that while they can steer and nurture the culture, they cannot dictate it. Culture is an organic entity shaped by the collective experiences and beliefs of the entire school community. Principals, therefore, must operate within this delicate balance of influence and inclusivity.

    A personal example from my time at one of my schools illustrates this dynamic vividly. I observed that students made no effort to engage with visitors or prospective parents during school tours, often not moving aside from their spaces during breaks to let visitors pass. This lack of courtesy not only reflected poorly on the school's culture but also diminished the overall visitor experience.

    Recognising the need for change, I took it upon myself to model the desired behaviours by entering the arena myself. Moving about the school, I engaged directly with students, greeting them and emphasising the importance of manners and acknowledgment. By introducing and reinforcing these small acts of courtesy, I demonstrated the behaviours we expected from our students.

    This approach not only transformed how students interacted with visitors but also highlighted the role of leadership in shaping school culture. My active participation and visibility among the students served as a powerful example, leading to a noticeable shift in student behaviour. Students began to mirror these actions, understanding that their engagement and manners were crucial to the school's identity and perception by outsiders.

    Through this initiative, we not only improved our school's hospitality but also strengthened our community's values, demonstrating the significant impact of leading by example in cultivating a positive and inclusive school culture.

2. **Modelling desired behaviours** is one of the most potent tools in a principal's arsenal, allowing them to lead by example by embodying the values, attitudes, and behaviours they wish to see throughout the school. This approach, however, demands authenticity and consistency; disingenuous or sporadic demonstrations of these values can erode trust and undermine efforts to build a positive culture.

   In one of my schools, I sought not only to foster a culture of inclusivity but also to enhance our students' public speaking capabilities, particularly for student leaders at assemblies and other public events. To achieve this, I modelled the speaking skills I wanted our students to develop. I made it a point to speak without notes, engaging the audience with keen eye contact, using exaggerated gestures, and maintaining a strong presence through confident body language. I kept my speeches to five minutes or less and frequently used humour to engage my audience. This visible demonstration of effective public speaking had a significant impact. Over time, students began to adopt these techniques, and their capacity to speak publicly improved impressively, reflecting a deeper confidence and engagement during school events.

   Alongside improving public speaking, I also focused on everyday interactions to enhance inclusivity. Each morning, I greeted students and staff personally, demonstrating my commitment to approachability and recognition of every individual. Furthermore, I attended and actively participated in various cultural events organised by different student groups, celebrating the diversity within our school community.

   However, in our pursuit of inclusivity within educational leadership, it is essential to reflect on implementing these values comprehensively. While it is commendable to see principals championing inclusivity, especially for minority and underrepresented groups, there appears to be an unintentional oversight in some cases.

   This oversight often pertains to the involvement of all stakeholders, including those who might be considered part of the traditional or majority groups, in significant decision-making processes. It is crucial to recognise that true inclusivity encompasses all school community members. In some instances, it has been observed that while there is a vocal and visible commitment to inclusivity, it does not always extend to collaborative practices with key leaders within the schools.

True inclusivity should be about advocating for the underrepresented and ensuring that everyone, irrespective of their background or status, is part of the dialogue and decision-making. This balanced approach is vital for fostering a genuinely inclusive and harmonious school environment.

3. **Fostering inclusive participation** is a key element in building a positive school culture and cannot be accomplished by the principal alone. To truly empower every member of the school community, principals must actively engage in practices that promote openness and collaboration. This means not only encouraging input from all quarters but also ensuring that this input is genuinely considered and valued in decision-making processes.

Here are some specific strategies that I used to foster an environment of inclusive participation:

- **Facilitate regular open forums.** I organised regular meetings where students, teachers, and staff could openly discuss their ideas, concerns, and suggestions.
- **Implement transparent communication channels.** I developed multiple, accessible channels for communication where community members could express their thoughts anonymously if they chose. I mainly used surveys.
- **Provide leadership training and development.** I offered training programs that helped develop leadership skills among students and staff. I met regularly with the school captains and every session included a "Leadership 101".
- **Model inclusive behaviour.** Perhaps most importantly to me, I modelled the inclusive behaviour I wanted to see. This involved more than just listening; it meant actively seeking out diverse viewpoints, being open to changing my perspectives, and demonstrating empathy and respect in every interaction.

By implementing these strategies, principals can transform the culture of their school into one where every member feels truly empowered to contribute. This creates a vibrant, dynamic environment where the collective wisdom and creativity of the school community drives continuous improvement and innovation.

4. **Navigating cultural change.** The role of a principal in navigating cultural change is akin to that of a skilled captain steering a ship through uncharted waters. While they hold the wheel, they must remain acutely aware of the currents and winds – the underlying dynamics of the school's culture. Principals must read these subtleties and respond with sensitivity and adaptability.

   Upon beginning my principalship at a new school, I was immediately met with a wave of concern from parents who expressed deep dissatisfaction with the school's standards and culture. Their criticisms were sharp and clear – they viewed our school as akin to "a public school that charged high fees". Though not intended as an affront to public schools, this phrase was their way of saying that the fees they paid did not reflect the standards and culture they expected. This feedback was a crucial wake-up call and set the stage for what would become a transformative journey in rebuilding the school's culture.

To address this challenge, I employed three critical strategies:

1. **Engaging all stakeholders in open dialogue.** Understanding that rebuilding culture is not a top-down process, I initiated open forums for dialogue among students, staff, and parents. These sessions provided a platform for everyone to voice their concerns, hopes, and visions for the school. This inclusive approach helped identify the key issues and fostered a sense of community and shared purpose in the cultural rebuilding process.

2. **Setting a clear vision and communicating it consistently.** I worked with the school leadership team to develop a clear, achievable vision for the school's culture. This vision was then communicated consistently across all platforms and interactions. By articulating what we aspired to become and tying every policy and decision back to this vision, we provided a clear roadmap for change and a benchmark for measuring progress.

   As I have discussed in earlier chapters, a good example of setting a clear vision and communicating it consistently was the process of becoming an IB World School, where I worked with the school leadership team to develop a clear, achievable vision for the school's culture. This vision was then communicated consistently across all platforms and interactions. By articulating what we aspired to become and tying every policy and decision back to this vision, we provided a clear roadmap for change and a benchmark for measuring progress.

3. **Leading by example and empowering change agents.** As the principal, I understood the importance of modelling our desired culture's behaviours and attitudes. Additionally, I identified and empowered teachers and students who showed the potential to be change agents within the school. By recognising and supporting these individuals, we created a network of cultural ambassadors who played a crucial role in driving and sustaining change throughout the school.

We embarked on a comprehensive initiative to elevate our standards and realign our culture with the expectations of our community. This involved revising policies and practices and nurturing a renewed sense of pride and excellence among students, staff, and parents. The journey was challenging, but by fostering open communication, setting clear goals, and working collaboratively, we successfully reshaped the school's culture, aligning it with the high standards our community rightfully expected.

3.4 Assessing school culture

Understanding and assessing the culture of my school was a complex yet essential task that I undertook as an educational leader. A healthy school culture not only fosters a positive learning environment but also enhances student achievement and supports staff well-being. In this subchapter, I explore various tools and methods that I employed to evaluate the health and effectiveness of my school's culture, providing actionable insights into how these assessments were conducted.

1. **Conducting comprehensive surveys.** I found surveys to be one of the most effective tools for gauging the perspectives of students, staff, and parents on various aspects of our school culture. I carefully designed these surveys to cover a range of topics, including attitudes towards learning, relationships among students and staff, feelings of safety and inclusivity, and satisfaction with the school environment. Analysing the results of these surveys gave me quantitative data that helped identify areas of strength and opportunities for improvement.
2. **Organising focus groups.** Focus groups offered a more qualitative approach to assessing our school culture. By bringing together small groups of students, teachers, or parents, I facilitated discussions that probed deeper into the nuances of the school's culture. These sessions were particularly valuable for exploring complex issues that surveys

may not fully capture, such as the dynamics of student–teacher relationships or the impact of recent changes within the school.
3. **Implementing classroom observations.** Classroom observations provided direct insights into the daily interactions and behaviours that shaped our school culture. By observing classes, I gathered firsthand information on teaching methods, student engagement, classroom management, and the overall learning environment. I ensured these observations were conducted regularly and systematically to maintain a comprehensive understanding of the school's academic culture.
4. **Analysing school performance data.** School performance data, such as attendance rates, disciplinary records, and academic outcomes, served as indirect indicators of our school culture. For instance, high absenteeism or frequent disciplinary issues often signalled a disengaged or unsettled school environment. Conversely, strong academic performance and high levels of participation in extracurricular activities indicated a positive and vibrant school culture.

Through these methods, I was able to gain a thorough understanding of the existing culture at my school and implement strategies that targeted specific areas for improvement, ultimately fostering a more positive and productive environment for everyone involved.

Case study – building culture over a glass of wine and a meal

In a bid to foster a deeper connection and understanding between the school and our parent community, I initiated a novel approach – hosting monthly dinners. Each dinner welcomed parents from five different families, along with a member of the school board and three staff members. Set in a warm and inviting atmosphere, these gatherings provided a unique platform for open dialogue and engagement. I took the opportunity to share the school's financials, discuss our future direction, and highlight the real and tangible benefits that our students were reaping from our school system.

The idea of sharing the finances was met with some consternation from directors who were concerned that this would be sharing too much (sensitive) information. However, the board chair attended the first dinner and she provided a glowing endorsement. And so I had the "green light". Parents loved it!

We engaged in earnest conversations over a shared meal and a glass of wine, actively seeking feedback and suggestions about the school. The parents were not just heard but listened to, making them feel valued and part of our school's journey. This strategy turned out to be incredibly effective.

Parents appreciated these evenings of candid conversation and felt a stronger connection to the school's mission and decisions. The success of these dinners was evident, and they became a much-anticipated event, continuing for two years as we cycled through all families who were interested in participating. This initiative not only strengthened our community bonds but also provided invaluable insights that helped shape a more responsive and inclusive school culture.

Assessing school culture is a multifaceted process that requires a combination of quantitative and qualitative methods. Surveys, focus groups, classroom observations, and the analysis of school performance data each offer unique insights into the health and effectiveness of a school's culture. By utilising these tools, principals can gain a comprehensive understanding of their school's culture, identifying areas of success as well as those in need of attention and improvement.

3.5 Addressing cultural disruptions

Dealing with cultural disruptions swiftly and effectively is critical in maintaining a healthy school culture. This can be managed through clear communication channels that allow issues to be reported and addressed promptly.

Training for staff on how to recognise and respond to signs of cultural discord is vital. For instance, holding regular meetings where staff can discuss cultural dynamics openly and propose solutions can help address issues before they escalate.

Moreover, having a clear set of community guidelines that outline acceptable behaviours and the consequences of cultural disruptions ensures that all members of the school community understand their roles in sustaining a positive culture.

3.6 Nurturing staff engagement and development

The vitality of a school's culture is significantly influenced by the engagement and development of its staff. In this subchapter, I explore the critical role of staff engagement in cultivating a positive school culture and present actionable insights into how this can be achieved through professional development, recognition programs, and staff wellness initiatives. Additionally, I will discuss the importance of promptly addressing behaviours that may be detrimental to the school's culture and morale.

Promoting professional development. One of the cornerstones of fostering staff engagement is providing ample opportunities for professional growth. This commitment extended beyond traditional development programs and involved creating a supportive environment where teachers and staff could pursue diverse educational opportunities.

Study abroad

In line with this, we introduced an innovative program that offered teachers and leaders short-term study-abroad opportunities. This program, made possible through the generosity of a silent benefactor, covered the costs of travel, accommodation, transfers, and study expenses for the staff members selected. The experiences gained from these international educational excursions were invaluable, not just in terms of professional learning but also in broadening cultural perspectives and fostering global connections.

By investing in their professional development in such a unique and expansive way, the school not only enhanced the skills and knowledge of its staff but also conveyed a strong message of value and respect for their contributions. I maintained a policy of rarely saying no to any reasonable request from staff for professional development. Whether it was attending workshops, participating in collaborative learning experiences, or embarking on international study tours, we ensured that our staff had access to a wide array of learning opportunities. This approach underpinned our belief that our staff's professional growth was integral to advancing our school as a whole, cultivating a culture where learning, innovation, and personal development were deeply valued.

Implementing recognition programs. This is a powerful strategy for acknowledging and appreciating staff members' hard work and achievements. These programs can range from formal award ceremonies to simple gestures of gratitude, each playing a critical role in boosting morale and reinforcing the behaviours and attitudes that align with the school's cultural values.

In my own experience, I integrated recognition into the customs of our school culture by purposefully including acknowledgment at all staff professional development (PD) days. As part of my welcome and opening remarks at the start of each term, I made it a point to highlight explicit examples of the great work performed by staff, teams, and individuals. This was not a perfunctory gesture but a sincere effort to celebrate the achievements across the entire spectrum of our school's staff – from teaching personnel to administrative and support teams.

By making this recognition inclusive of all employees and teams, I ensured that everyone felt valued and recognised, regardless of their role. This practice helped to build a stronger, more cohesive community and encouraged a culture of ongoing excellence and mutual respect. Such acknowledgments not only validated the hard work of our staff but also served as a motivating factor for others to strive for similar recognition, thereby fostering a positive and supportive work environment where every contribution is noticed and celebrated.

Prioritising staff well-being. The well-being of staff is integral to maintaining a positive school culture. Initiatives focusing on physical, mental, and emotional wellness promote a healthy work environment. This can include access to counselling services, fitness programs, and work–life balance policies. A staff that feels cared for is more likely to be engaged and committed to the school's mission.

I didn't have one particular program that I could attest to as "gold" star. I wanted to provide a range of opportunities that could potentially meet the needs of every staff member, whose individual needs were quite different.

- We had occasional workshops – topics included stress management, emotional resilience, and effective communication skills.
- On-site yoga and aerobics were offered before and after school hours.
- We provided regular health assessments including blood-pressure checks, cholesterol tests, and mental health screenings.
- Free access to qualified counsellors and psychologists was available during and after school hours, including virtual sessions.
- We held regularly scheduled events such as staff outings, family days, and cultural celebrations to strengthen community ties.

Addressing cultural disruptions with alacrity is an essential part of my leadership approach, emphasising the importance of maintaining the integrity of school culture. Whenever I observed a staff member behaving in a manner that threatened to damage our culture or reduce the morale of others, I acted with alacrity and speed. Addressing such issues promptly and effectively was crucial in preserving the positive atmosphere and mutual respect that are the bedrock of a school community. This decisiveness not only helped rectify immediate issues but also set a precedent for the type of conduct expected and valued within our school.

To further enhance engagement and bring staff members back into the fold, particularly after incidents that may have caused friction or disengagement, I gave the staff member the opportunity to provide feedback that allowed them to voice concerns and offer suggestions in a constructive manner. This approach not only facilitated open communication but also demonstrated that their opinions were valued and could lead to real change.

Additionally, I prioritised regular check-ins with staff, creating spaces where they could discuss their professional journeys and personal well-being in a supportive environment. These check-ins were not only about performance but also about personal growth and satisfaction, which helped to re-engage staff who might have felt overlooked or undervalued.

Through these practices, coupled with a consistent focus on professional development and recognition, I aimed to nurture a culture where every staff member felt cared for and invested in our collective mission. These efforts to engage and develop staff were not just administrative tasks; they were crucial strategies that reinforced our school's values and mission, ultimately creating a more cohesive and motivated team. These strategies not only contributed to a positive working and educational environment but also resonated through every aspect of school life, positively impacting students and the broader school community.

3.7 Student-centric cultural practices

Recognising and incorporating student perspectives into the framework of school culture is paramount. A student-centric approach ensures that the culture of a school resonates with those at its very heart – the students themselves. This involves more than just acknowledging their presence; it requires actively engaging with their unique needs, aspirations, and perspectives to create an environment that truly reflects and supports their educational journey.

The key to this approach is offering substantial student leadership opportunities. By empowering students to take on meaningful roles within the school community, they not only develop essential leadership skills but also gain a sense of ownership and responsibility towards their school environment. This empowerment leads to a more dynamic and inclusive school culture, one that is shaped by the diverse voices of its student body.

Incorporating student feedback in decision-making processes is another critical aspect. Regular surveys, suggestion boxes, and open forums encourage students to voice their opinions and ideas. This feedback becomes an invaluable tool for school leaders, providing insights into the effectiveness of current practices and highlighting areas for improvement. By prioritising student voices in this manner, the school culture becomes a collaborative creation, continuously evolving to meet the changing needs of its student community.

Real-life example

To create a student-centric culture, I placed a special emphasis on connecting with student leaders. One of the most effective ways I found to do this was through weekly morning tea sessions with the school captains. These gatherings were informal yet structured, providing a relaxed atmosphere for open and honest dialogue. During these meetings, I imparted a light-touch version of Leadership 101, sharing insights and experiences from my own journey to help them develop their skills.

But these sessions were more than just about leadership lessons; they were a two-way street. I actively sought the captains' support on school-wide matters, valuing their input and perspectives. These discussions often brought to light what was working well within the school and, importantly, what wasn't. Their feedback was a vital resource, helping me focus my energy and efforts on areas that needed attention. By regularly engaging with the school captains in this manner, I not only gained valuable insights into the student experience but also fostered a sense of collaboration and mutual respect. This approach reinforced the idea that our students were not just learners but integral contributors to the school culture.

3.8 Faith and cultural dynamics in schools

In faith-based schools, the embedded religious beliefs significantly shape the educational and cultural environment. The impact of these beliefs on school culture cannot be underestimated, as they often dictate the values, traditions, and behaviours within the school community.

For example, Jewish and Muslim schools not only incorporate religious studies into their curriculum but also ensure that daily practices and school operations adhere to their faith's teachings. This integration extends to the roles of rabbis and imams, who contribute not just as spiritual leaders but also as cultural stewards.

Understanding and respecting these religious nuances is crucial in such settings, as it influences teaching methods, student interactions, and community engagement. Schools must navigate these cultural complexities with sensitivity and an inclusive approach, ensuring that while faith forms the core of the culture, it also embraces diversity within the faith community.

3.9 Engaging with parents and the community

In building a thriving school culture, the engagement of parents and the community plays a pivotal role. However, this engagement, if not managed correctly, can also become a source of what I term "culture killers" – factors that can significantly undermine the positive culture we strive to build within our schools. Based on my experiences, I've identified the top three culture killers in relation to parental engagement, each requiring careful navigation and strategy.

One culture killer is the "echo chamber effect". This occurs when a small group of vocal parents dominate conversations, often in parent-teacher meetings or school forums, leading to a skewed representation of the broader parent body's views. Their repeated and loud opinions can overshadow diverse perspectives, creating an environment where only certain viewpoints are heard and amplified.

In one of my schools where parents were particularly vocal about the school's philosophies, I had to combat the echo chamber effect and ensure a more equitable representation of the broader parent body. I introduced a structured feedback mechanism known as the "Parent Insight Panel". This panel of five parents was designed to gather a diverse group of parents from various backgrounds and grade levels, rotating members regularly to avoid dominance by any single group or perspective.

The Parent Insight Panel met quarterly, providing a structured environment where parents could express their concerns, suggestions, and feedback directly to school leadership. I used the panel to ask questions about community "noise" and strategic changes that I was thinking about.

This approach not only diversified the range of voices heard but also provided a clear, formal avenue for engagement that discouraged the dominance of any single group. By democratising the discourse in this way, the school was better able to address concerns genuinely reflective of the entire community, rather than being swayed by a vocal minority.

Another significant culture killer I addressed was "helicopter parenting". Overly involved parents can inadvertently stifle the growth and independence of students by being too present and too interventionist in their child's school life. This behaviour can disrupt the learning environment and hinder our learners' development of crucial life skills.

To address this, I initiated a strategy that involved inviting parents into the school to share in their children's learning and social activities, but in a structured and formal way. This approach aimed to channel their involvement positively without allowing it to become disruptive. For instance, we organised "Parent Observation Days" where parents were invited to observe classes, but they were asked to follow specific guidelines to minimise disturbances to the teaching environment. These guidelines included silent observation and saving questions for the end of the session, where they could engage with teachers during a designated Q&A time.

Additionally, our junior school, led by the head of primary, implemented a family learning project that incorporated the "Eco-Adventure Challenge". This project aimed to combine physical education with environmental science in a family-oriented activity.

The Eco-Adventure Challenge involved families working together to complete a series of outdoor activities that were both fun and educational. The challenge was structured around a scavenger hunt held within the school grounds, where families followed clues to locate various checkpoints. At each checkpoint, there were activities or questions related to environmental science, such as identifying native plant species, calculating the age of trees, or completing tasks that demonstrated sustainable practices like recycling or water conservation.

Parents and children were encouraged to work together to solve problems and complete physical tasks, which included light jogging between checkpoints, using a compass, and performing team exercises that required cooperation and communication. The event not only promoted physical fitness but also offered an engaging way for families to learn about environmental stewardship together.

By creating a structured yet enjoyable setting for family participation, the Eco-Adventure Challenge ensured that parents could contribute positively to their children's learning experiences without compromising their independence. This project fostered a sense of community among families and provided a practical application of school lessons in a real-world setting, enhancing both physical health and environmental awareness.

Through these initiatives, we successfully balanced the need for parental involvement with the necessity of fostering an educational environment conducive to developing independent, resilient students. This approach not only mitigated the negative impacts of helicopter parenting but also reinforced a culture of constructive and appropriate engagement.

Another culture killer is the **lack of transparent communication**. When parents are not kept informed or feel excluded from the school's discourse, mistrust can develop. This mistrust erodes the foundation of a healthy school–community relationship. It is essential to establish clear, open communication channels, ensuring that parents feel informed and heard. Regular updates, open meetings, and responsive communication channels can help bridge this gap, building trust and a sense of partnership.

Another culture killer is the **perception of indifference to parental concerns**. When parents feel that their opinions or worries are disregarded, it can lead to a sense of disenfranchisement. To counter this, it is important to create platforms where parents can voice their concerns and feel assured they are being considered. This could be through parent–teacher meetings, feedback forms, or community forums.

Lastly, a **lack of visible community involvement** in the school can dampen the spirit of collective responsibility and pride. Schools thrive when they are seen as integral parts of the community. Inviting community members to participate in school events, engaging in community projects, and creating partnership programs with local businesses or organisations can infuse a sense of shared purpose and collaboration.

By addressing these culture killers head-on, schools can create an environment where parents and the community are not just spectators but active participants in the educational journey. This inclusive approach not only enriches the school culture but also creates a supportive network that extends far beyond the school gates, laying the groundwork for a thriving educational ecosystem.

The tale of Principal RB and the community connection

Once in a small town, there was a school led by a principal (I won't use their name) known for her sharp mind and dedication. Principal RB often found herself buried in paperwork and administrative duties in her office. However, her presence on the school grounds and at community events was noticeably lacking, a fact that did not go unnoticed among parents and staff.

Whispers of her absence turned into cynical remarks. "She's more a ghost than a principal," some would say. "I bet she doesn't even know what happens during recess," others would quip.

She would be conspicuous by her absence at important celebrations and ceremonies, and when she did attend, she would not speak.

Then came the annual spring fair, an event where the school traditionally played a significant role. Principal RB had a unique opportunity presented to her. She could do one of two things. Continue to lead through conspicuous absence or take a new approach and lead by her active presence. The fair was an opportunity for Principal RB to step out of her office, leave behind the towering piles of paperwork, and join her school in the festival preparations. What did she choose to do?

To the surprise of many, she didn't just oversee; she actively participated. She helped the art teacher with the decorations, joined the students in rehearsals for the school play, and even volunteered at the community food drive booth.

Her involvement brought a refreshing change. Parents and teachers saw a different side of her – one that was approachable, involved, and deeply caring. Conversations began to change. "Did you see Principal RB helping out with the costumes?" "She was planning the food drive with the students at the hall!"

This change in Principal RB rippled through the school. Seeing her engage so actively, staff and students felt renewed collective responsibility and pride. They realised that their school was more than just a building – it was a vital part of their community.

Emboldened by this newfound spirit, Principal RB initiated more community involvement activities. She invited local business owners to mentor students, collaborated with community leaders on educational projects, and opened the school grounds for community events.

Principal RB, who was once perceived as a distant authority figure, transformed into a beloved community pillar through her active participation in such initiatives. She didn't just oversee the events but also participated alongside families, embodying the spirit of involvement and collaboration she aimed to instil in her school culture. *In other words, she truly rolled up her sleeves!* This shift in her approach not only brought her closer to the community but also set a powerful example of leadership by engagement.

3.10 Sustaining a dynamic school culture

Sustaining a dynamic school culture is an ongoing journey that requires both attentiveness and adaptability. One effective yet often overlooked strategy I employed was being present in the school car park at the start and end of each day. This custom is carried out by many principals and heads of sub-schools every day across the country. This simple act provided a unique vantage point for me to observe and engage with the school's culture in its most unfiltered form. The car park was where daily greetings were exchanged, where the anxieties and excitement of students were most visible, and where informal yet insightful conversations with parents often took place.

Such direct engagement offered real-time insights into the health of our school culture. It allowed me to gauge the mood and morale of students and staff, providing clues on areas where the school was thriving and aspects that might need more attention. Moreover, this presence in the car park helped foster a sense of approachability and openness, signalling to the school community that their experiences and perspectives were valued and that leadership was accessible and responsive.

Balancing this hands-on approach with continuous assessment and adaptation of cultural practices ensured that our school culture remained vibrant and responsive. It was about more than just implementing formal strategies; it was about being actively present in the school's daily life, ready to listen, observe, and adapt. In doing so, the school culture remained a concept discussed in meetings and a lived and continuously evolving experience for everyone in the school community.

Adaptation is equally vital. In a world where change is the only constant, a school culture that remains rigidly fixed is bound to become irrelevant. This requires a leadership mindset that is not just open to change but actively seeks it. It involves being courageous enough to let go of outdated traditions and bold enough to embrace new ideas that resonate with the current and future generations of the school community.

Sustaining a dynamic school culture is about striking a balance between honouring the school's heritage and embracing the possibilities of the future. It's about creating a culture that is not just surviving but thriving, constantly rejuvenating itself to remain a vibrant, engaging, and inspiring place for learning and growth.

3.11 Key takeaways

Here are the key takeaways from this chapter on building and sustaining a positive school culture.

Each point serves as a foundational pillar for fostering an environment where every member of the school community – students, staff, and parents alike – feels valued and engaged.

1. **Active engagement.** Regular, meaningful interaction with all members of the school community – students, staff, and parents – is essential. Presence in everyday settings like the car park can offer valuable insights.
2. **Continuous assessment and adaptation.** Regularly evaluate the school culture through surveys, observations, and feedback, and be willing to adapt practices to meet evolving needs.
3. **Empowering leadership.** Lead by example and empower others, including student leaders and staff, to actively shape the school culture.
4. **Open communication.** Maintain transparent and open lines of communication with all stakeholders, ensuring that everyone feels heard and valued.
5. **Community involvement.** Engage with the wider community to extend the school's cultural reach and foster a sense of shared responsibility and pride.
6. **Addressing culture killers.** Be vigilant about identifying and addressing behaviours or practices that can negatively impact school culture. Silent quitting is one problem that can go undetected for a while; it needs to be surfaced and addressed.
7. **Student-centric approach.** Prioritise student voices in decision-making to ensure the culture remains relevant and supports their needs.
8. **Staff development and well-being.** Invest in the professional development and well-being of staff, recognising their critical role in fostering a positive school culture.
9. **Celebrating successes.** Acknowledge and celebrate the achievements and improvements within the school, reinforcing a culture of appreciation and positivity.

To conclude, using the words of the highly respected world leader Nelson Mandela: "Education is the most powerful weapon which you can use to change the world." This profound statement resonates deeply with the theme of this chapter, highlighting the pivotal role that school culture plays in education. A robust and positive school culture doesn't just facilitate learning; it shapes the mindset and capabilities of future generations, preparing them to make meaningful contributions to society.

By nurturing an environment where values, traditions, and behaviours align to support and enhance educational outcomes, we are essentially equipping students with the tools they need to change the world. Thus, Mandela's insight encapsulates the overarching goal of cultivating a school culture that not only enriches students within the school walls but also empowers them to shape the future of our society.

CHAPTER 4

NAVIGATING THE SEAS OF CHANGE

Change management and innovation in education

4.1 Understanding the nature of change in education

As a leader who has often been described as a change leader and restless in pursuit of improvement, I have personally experienced the relentless pace of transformation in education. My philosophy has always been grounded in the belief that one must embody the spirit of change to provide a relevant and contemporary education. This belief stems not from a mere preference for novelty but from a deep-seated conviction that stagnation in educational practices risks rendering our teaching irrelevant in the face of rapidly evolving societal and technological landscapes.

My journey has been one of constant adaptation, always seeking to understand and anticipate shifts in the educational paradigm. It's a journey driven by the understanding that, as educators and leaders, we are not just imparting knowledge but are shaping the future, and growing adults. In embracing change, we ensure that our students are equipped for today's world and tomorrow's uncharted territories.

This perspective has informed my approach to leadership in education. It is about more than keeping pace with change; it is about being a step ahead and proactively shaping the educational landscape. By fostering an environment where change is not only expected but eagerly anticipated, we can cultivate a generation of learners and educators who are resilient, adaptable, and prepared for the inevitable shifts that the future holds.

Much like the world it prepares us for, education is in a constant state of evolution. Recognising and embracing the inevitability of change is beneficial and essential for those who lead and shape the future of learning. This subchapter explores the multifaceted nature of change in the educational landscape, exploring how technological advancements, evolving pedagogical theories, and societal shifts collectively drive the continuous transformation of education.

Change in education is far from a recent trend. Throughout history, educational systems have continually evolved to meet societal demands. A prime example from my experience is the introduction of the Texas Instruments calculator in the 1970s, a game-changer for schools and learners alike. I remember the excitement and curiosity permeating classrooms as we explored this new technology. It marked a significant shift, similar to the earlier introduction of compulsory schooling and the later integration of digital technologies into learning environments.

Recently, however, the pace of change has been unprecedented, driven by rapid technological advances and a deeper understanding of pedagogical processes. Witnessing and participating in this swift evolution firsthand has been both exhilarating and challenging. Educators and leaders must be perpetually adaptable, embracing new tools, methodologies, and expectations to stay relevant and effective in our ever-evolving educational landscape.

Technological innovation stands at the forefront of this change. Technology integration in education has revolutionised how we teach and learn. From the use of interactive whiteboards to the implementation of learning management systems, technology has expanded the horizons of educational possibilities. It facilitates personalised learning experiences, breaks down geographical barriers, and provides access to an immense wealth of information. However, it also brings challenges, such as the need for digital literacy, the digital divide, and ensuring equitable access to technological resources. As I write this chapter – Happy first birthday ChatGPT! It was 30 November 2022 when Open AI released ChatGPT 3.5. It has been a big, wild year, and the impact on education has been enormous.

Equally important is the shift in pedagogical theories. Education today is not just about imparting knowledge; it is about fostering critical thinking, creativity, and adaptability. Contemporary pedagogical approaches emphasise student-centred learning, where the focus is on developing skills and competencies that prepare learners for a rapidly changing world. This shift requires educators to continuously update their teaching strategies, moving from traditional lecture-based methods to more interactive, collaborative, and inquiry-based approaches.

Moreover, societal changes play a significant role in shaping education. The increasing cultural diversity in classrooms, changing family dynamics, and evolving societal norms necessitate an education system that is inclusive, sensitive, and responsive to a wide range of needs and backgrounds.

Auburn High School in Melbourne, Victoria, for example, has a diverse student population, with students coming from families with heritage in over 50 different countries. Auburn High School, like many other schools in cosmopolitan areas of Australia, reflects the country's rich cultural diversity. This diversity provides a unique educational environment where students not only learn from their curriculums but also gain invaluable insights and understanding from their peers of different cultural backgrounds. Such schools are microcosms of Australia's multicultural society, offering students the opportunity to develop global awareness and cultural sensitivity from a young age.

The example of Auburn High School offers a valuable lesson on the benefits of embracing cultural diversity within schools. Here are a few key insights we can learn from students from multicultural backgrounds.

- **Enhanced cultural sensitivity.** Students exposed to a wide array of cultural perspectives enrich their understanding and appreciation of different customs, traditions, and viewpoints. This exposure helps cultivate a level of cultural sensitivity that is vital in today's globalised world.
- **Global awareness.** By interacting with peers from diverse backgrounds, students develop a broader world view. This global awareness is an essential skill, equipping students to operate effectively and empathetically in diverse settings, whether in further education, the workplace, or social environments.
- **Mutual respect and inclusion.** Schools with diverse populations serve as important arenas for teaching mutual respect and the value of inclusion. Students learn to appreciate differences and recognise the strength that comes from a diverse community.

- **Preparation for global opportunities.** As students from multicultural environments venture into the world, their early experiences of diversity prepare them for the global opportunities and challenges they might face in their personal and professional lives.

Understanding the nature of change in education requires acknowledging that change is not an isolated event but a constant process. It demands a proactive approach, where educators and administrators are not just reacting to changes but anticipating and preparing for them. This involves staying informed about emerging trends, being open to innovation, and fostering a culture of continuous learning and adaptation.

As we explore the various facets of change in the educational landscape, it becomes evident that *the only constant in education is change itself.* By understanding and embracing this, educators and leaders can better prepare themselves and their students for the dynamic and ever-evolving future that lies ahead.

4.2 Identifying drivers of change

Change in education is not random or arbitrary; it is driven by various factors that continuously shape and reshape the educational landscape. Understanding these drivers is crucial for educators and leaders to anticipate and effectively plan for change. Here are some key drivers of change in education, along with a brief commentary on each:

1. **New research findings.** Educational methodologies evolve with new research into how we learn. Advances in cognitive science, psychology, and educational theory often lead to shifts in teaching practices, emphasising more effective or engaging methods.
2. **Societal needs.** As society changes, so do the required skills and knowledge. Today's education must prepare students for a world that values digital literacy, environmental awareness, and global citizenship, among other contemporary needs.
3. **Policy shifts.** Education policies significantly impact how education is delivered, whether at the local, national, or international level. Changes in funding, curriculum standards, assessment methods, and accountability measures can prompt significant adjustments in educational institutions.
4. **Technological innovations.** Technology continually revolutionises education. From the rise of e-learning platforms to AI-driven

personalised learning, technology changes how we teach and expands what can be taught and how students engage with the material.

5. **Economic factors.** Economic trends can influence education in multiple ways, from impacting government spending on education to shifting job market demands, thereby influencing what skills and knowledge are prioritised in curricula.
6. **Cultural and social dynamics.** Cultural shifts, such as increasing diversity and changing family structures, influence educational priorities and approaches. Education must adapt to be inclusive and responsive to these diverse backgrounds and experiences.
7. **Global events.** Large-scale events like Covid-19, climate change, and political upheavals have profound effects on education, necessitating rapid adaptation and resilience.

Recognising and understanding these drivers is pivotal for educators to stay informed and prepared. This proactive approach allows educators to react to changes and influence and shape them, ensuring that education remains relevant, effective, and forward-thinking.

Professional networks

I want to highlight a crucial driver of change – the need for broader professional networks and exposure to diverse educational perspectives.

The need for broader professional networks and exposure to diverse educational perspectives is driven by the demand for innovation, effective problem-solving, adaptability to global trends, ongoing professional development, enhanced cultural competence, and stronger influence in educational policy and advocacy. These factors are essential for educators looking to lead and succeed in the dynamic field of education.

A key driver of change at one of my schools was the pressing need to *broaden the professional networks of our teachers*. Previously, our educational community was primarily local-centric, predominantly engaging with professionals within a rural city of about 50,000 people. This limited scope, while close-knit, risked becoming insular, as many educators had deep-rooted ties to the region, having grown up and trained there. Connecting our educators with colleagues in larger, more diverse schools became essential to invigorate our teaching practices and bring fresh perspectives.

The goal was to foster connections beyond our local community, extending to the nearest capital city of 4.5 million people, other states across Australia, and even an international network of educators. This expansion was not just about breaking free from a somewhat confined educational echo chamber but was also about embracing a multitude of teaching methodologies, educational innovations, and diverse experiences. By tapping into this wider network, our teachers could benefit from a richer web of professional development opportunities and collaborative learning experiences, enhancing their skills and bringing new ideas and approaches back to our local context.

This approach to broadening professional networks underscores the importance of exposure to varied educational contexts and the value of learning from a diverse array of educators. It represents a strategic shift towards a more open and globally connected educational practice.

4.3 The role of leadership in change management

At the very heart of educational innovation stands leadership – not just any leadership, but one that dares to provoke, inspire, and conduct. What is the visceral reality of what it truly means to be an educational leader during times of significant change? It is not for the faint-hearted; it is for the bold, the brave, those who are ready to orchestrate the symphony of change.

Imagine standing as the conductor of a world-class orchestra. That is what leading an educational institution through change feels like. It is complex, nuanced, and exhilarating. The first step? Setting a vision that's not just a distant echo but a vivid, compelling composition of what could be. This vision isn't pulled out of thin air; it is meticulously composed from the raw, unvarnished truths of what education needs to become.

What value does a vision hold without an orchestra ready to perform? Motivation lies not in merely directing or instructing but in igniting a passion within each musician. Leadership involves inspiring team members to see themselves as virtuosos in a grand ensemble rather than just individual performers. The goal is to instil a profound belief in their essential role in this ambitious concert. And then comes orchestrating the strategic direction – the part where true skill is tested. This isn't just a routine rehearsal; it is a masterful performance through complex compositions, requiring bold decisions, often made amidst a cacophony of diverse opinions. It means sometimes rewriting the score and leading the ensemble through uncharted musical territories. It is about being fearless in facing the crescendos, challenging the musical status quo, and sometimes standing alone on the podium, directing the ensemble with unshakeable resolve towards a grand finale.

Effective leadership in these times is about being not just a foundation of stability but the conductor who guides the orchestra through a long and intense piece. It involves embracing the ebb and flow of change, and understanding that the tide of education is a relentless force, constantly shaping and reshaping the landscape.

In the end, the role of a leader in change management is not just about managing change; it is about embodying it, living it, and leading it. It is a journey of constant learning, unlearning, and relearning. It is about being audacious enough to dismantle the old, wise enough to cherish the valuable, and visionary enough to build the new. This is the nucleus of leadership in the crucible of change – not just navigating the ship but being the tide that reshapes education's shores.

In the pivotal journey of transforming our school into an IB World School, my role as the principal was marked by strategic foresight and dynamic leadership. Recognising the transformative potential of the IB framework, I embarked on a mission to not only embrace an internationally recognised educational standard but also foster a global mindset within our school community. This endeavour required more than mere administrative oversight; it demanded visionary leadership.

I led from the front, ensuring that every stakeholder understood and was aligned with the core values and objectives of the IB philosophy. This transition was not without its challenges; it required reshaping our curriculum, retraining our faculty, and reorienting our students and their families to a new way of learning and thinking. My leadership involved being the chief communicator, the primary motivator, and the steadfast navigator through this complex process. I facilitated extensive professional development for our teachers, fostering a culture of continuous learning and adaptation.

I kept the school community informed, involved, and inspired through town hall meetings, newsletters, and personal interactions. By articulating a clear vision, rallying the support of all stakeholders, and steering the school through the rigorous accreditation process, I ensured that our transition to an IB World School was not just a change in the curriculum but a meaningful evolution towards creating a more inclusive, global, and forward-thinking educational environment.

In the original phase of approving and confirming our last major program, the Diploma, the board underwent a dramatic and inexplicable shift in their approach. Previously, they had placed their trust in the school's executive leadership to make significant strategic operational decisions. However, they abruptly transitioned to a more corporatised governance style. This new approach mandated that a comprehensive business plan accompany every innovative idea or forward-thinking proposal. Such a requirement was unprecedented for this board and became a standard expectation, significantly hindering the agility and effectiveness of the school's leadership team. Perhaps this is the new norm in independent school governance.

While the capacity to navigate the treacherous seas of change is a celebrated trait of effective leadership, there is also profound wisdom in recognising moments of calm where consolidation is more beneficial than further change. This concept, which I refer to as "the art of smooth sailing", emphasises the importance of stability and the value of existing practices that are already successful.

Leaders must be wary of "change mania" – the compulsion to alter foundational elements simply to make one's mark, which can destabilise and demoralise a school community. A prime example can be observed in scenarios where new leaders, driven perhaps more by ego than by the school's actual needs, introduce radical changes without fully understanding the implications or valuing the established systems that work well.

Such leadership not only risks the integrity of well-functioning practices but can also lead to unnecessary upheaval that benefits no one. Instead, effective leadership involves discerning when to innovate and when to preserve, ensuring that change is meaningful and genuinely aligned with the school's long-term vision and health. It is crucial that leaders resist the urge to leave a personal imprint at the expense of the school's legacy, choosing instead to build upon the solid foundation already in place.

4.4 Engaging stakeholders in the change process – focusing on teachers

Teachers often stand as the most formidable stakeholders in the crucible of educational transformation. Their involvement in the change process is not just important; it is an absolute necessity, albeit challenging. This subchapter takes an unflinching look at the dynamic of involving teachers in change, acknowledging their frequent resistance to new methods yet emphasising their critical role.

Let's face it: teachers can be the staunchest guardians of the status quo. Their resistance to change isn't always a matter of stubbornness; it often stems from a deep-rooted commitment to their practices and a protective stance towards their students. However, this very resistance can turn teachers into disruptors when it comes to implementing change. So, how do we navigate this complex terrain?

The key lies in communication – not the sugar-coated, placating kind, but direct, honest communication and acknowledging the challenges up front. This means laying out the what, why, and how of the change in no uncertain terms. It involves showing teachers the hard facts and the potential impacts, making them see beyond the comfort of the familiar.

Collaboration is another critical strategy. This doesn't mean simply asking for their opinions; it means genuinely involving them in shaping the change. It is about harnessing their insights, their classroom experiences, and their concerns to refine and adapt the proposed changes. Yes, this approach is messier, and it takes longer, but it turns potential adversaries into allies.

Moreover, there's the need for a bit of tough love. Leaders must be prepared to challenge the mindsets that resist change. This involves calling out unfounded fears, dispelling myths, and sometimes, pushing teachers out of their comfort zones. It is not about being authoritarian but about being a catalyst for critical thinking and self-reflection among teachers.

Lastly, recognise and reward adaptability and innovation. Highlight those teachers who embrace change and demonstrate its benefits. Make them the champions of change, not as a token gesture, but as a genuine acknowledgment of their role in leading by example.

In short, engaging teachers in the change process is a balancing act. It requires a blend of empathy and firmness, collaboration and leadership, encouragement and challenge. It is about steering them away from being mere spectators or disruptors to becoming active participants in the journey of educational evolution. This process may not be smooth, but it is undeniably crucial for any meaningful and lasting change in education.

4.5 Cautionary tales

Caution against educational fads

While educators and leaders must be adaptable and open to innovation, it is equally important to approach new trends and methodologies with a critical eye.

The educational landscape, perhaps more than any other field, is susceptible to fads that may not be substantiated by solid research and can lead to suboptimal outcomes. Leaders must develop the ability to distinguish between genuine innovations that enhance learning and fleeting trends with little educational value. This involves a commitment to evidence-based practice – carefully reviewing the research, understanding the theoretical underpinnings, and considering the long-term implications before adopting new tools or methodologies.

A pragmatic approach to innovation can prevent the enthusiastic but uncritical adoption of new trends that fail to contribute meaningfully to educational goals.

Caution against human cost

As we embrace change and innovation in schools, it is crucial to conduct thorough human cost–benefit analyses to understand the broader implications of these initiatives.

Not all technological advancements are beneficial; some may inadvertently harm the very processes they intend to improve or disrupt crucial aspects of the learning environment. Educators should assess not only the potential benefits but also the possible disruptions caused by new technologies, ensuring that innovations serve to enhance rather than diminish the quality of education.

This balanced perspective helps safeguard against the unintended consequences of change, ensuring that technological integration is always aligned with educational values and the well-being of all stakeholders.

Caution on technological change

It is important to clarify that while I advocate for embracing technological advancements, my endorsement is not indiscriminate. The successful integration of technology in education should be thoughtful, purposeful, and, above all, educationally sound.

Leaders must distinguish between technologies that truly enhance teaching and learning and those that might undermine these processes. By fostering a culture that values thoughtful innovation over hasty adoption, we can ensure that technology serves as a tool for educational enhancement rather than a force for unnecessary disruption.

4.6 Managing resistance to change

Addressing resistance to change within schools is a complex and delicate process that demands a thoughtful combination of empathy, effective communication, and genuine involvement. Here is how I navigated and mitigated resistance to change, providing a guide that is both intuitive and straightforward.

Identifying the root causes of resistance – understanding why resistance occurs was crucial. Whether it stemmed from fear of the unknown, lack of trust, poor experiences with previous changes, or feelings of being undervalued, recognising these reasons allowed me to address them effectively. My tactics included:

1. **Structured interviews.** I conducted one-on-one interviews with staff members who expressed concerns about the proposed changes.
2. **Focus groups.** I organised focus groups with diverse cross-sections of our staff to discuss the changes. This setting often helped participants express and explore their views and hear others' perceptions and concerns.
3. **Direct observations.** During meetings where changes were discussed, I observed reactions and behaviours. Non-verbal cues and dynamics were very telling. I kept detailed notes on reactions and any resistance patterns that emerged, looking for triggers and commonalities.
4. **Transparent and frequent communication.** I maintained open and transparent communication channels. Regular updates about the changes, their necessity, and their benefits were crucial. I anticipated questions and concerns, addressing them proactively.
5. **Demonstrating empathy and understanding.** I showed understanding and empathy towards the concerns of my staff. Acknowledging that change can be challenging and unsettling, I reassured them that their feelings were valid and heard.
6. **Involving teachers in the change process.** Instead of imposing changes, I involved teachers in the process. I sought their input, suggestions, and feedback. When people felt they were part of the process, they were more likely to embrace the changes.
7. **Providing adequate training and support.** I ensured that our staff had the necessary training and resources to adapt to new changes. This included professional development sessions, workshops, and mentorship programs.
8. **Creating small wins and celebrating them.** I started with small, manageable changes to demonstrate the positive impacts of the

transformation. Celebrating these wins, no matter how small, helped build confidence and momentum.

9. **Leading by example.** As principal, my attitude towards change set the tone for the entire school. I stayed positive, resilient, and adaptable, showing my commitment to the changes through my actions and decisions.
10. **Fostering a culture of continuous improvement.** I encouraged a mindset where change was seen as an opportunity for growth and improvement. I cultivated an environment where feedback was valued and mistakes were viewed as learning opportunities.
11. **Monitoring progress and adjusting as necessary.** I regularly assessed how the change was being implemented and its impact. I was willing to make adjustments based on feedback and the results I observed.
12. **Recognising and rewarding adaptation.** I acknowledged and rewarded those who were adapting to the change. Recognition proved to be a powerful motivator for others to follow suit.

By employing these strategies, I aimed to manage and reduce resistance effectively, paving the way for a smoother transition and a more adaptive school culture.

Real-life example

While implementing transformative changes at our school, I encountered a particularly tricky leader, John, notorious for his passive resistance to new initiatives. Despite the apparent benefits, John remained a steadfast sceptic.

Undeterred, I engaged him directly, inviting him to one-on-one meetings where I listened earnestly to his concerns and perspectives. Recognising his deep-seated fear of the unfamiliar, I involved him in the planning stages of new projects, turning his scepticism into a valuable tool for identifying potential pitfalls. Gradually, John began to see the positive impacts of the changes firsthand. His involvement addressed his apprehensions and allowed him to contribute meaningfully, transforming him from a passive resister into a proactive advocate for change. His journey from scepticism to support became a powerful testament to the power of patient engagement and inclusive leadership. I am on his Christmas card list!

A principal can guide their school through the complexities of change with a focus on empathy, clear communication, and inclusive involvement, thus creating a smoother and more successful transition.

4.7 Implementing change successfully

The journey of successfully implementing change in an educational setting is both challenging and rewarding. A prime example of this in my experience was the ambitious project of building a comprehensive music centre and concert hall from scratch. This venture was not simply about erecting a building; it was about creating a vibrant hub for musical excellence where over 600 students would hone their skills, some reaching the heights of performing on national and international stages.

Setting clear objectives

The initial step was to crystallise our objectives. The goal was to establish a music centre that would serve as a state-of-the-art music education facility and a cultural pillar for the community. This involved planning the physical infrastructure and the program's scope, including curriculum development, performance opportunities, and community outreach initiatives.

Developing a detailed plan

With our objectives defined, detailed planning was essential. This included architectural designs for the music centre and concert hall, ensuring acoustical excellence, and a comprehensive budget covering construction, instruments, and operational costs. I also delineated a timeline for each phase, from groundbreaking to the grand opening.

Securing resources and funding

The realisation of our music centre and concert hall hinged significantly on securing adequate resources and funding. A crucial component of our funding strategy was to attract major donors whose contributions could provide a substantial portion of the needed capital. This task was formidable, requiring not just persuasive pitches, but a deep alignment with the donors' values and visions for community impact.

In this pursuit, the pivotal breakthrough came through securing the support of two major benefactors: Mick Power AM and the John T Reid Charitable Trusts. Their generous gifts were not just financial injections but powerful endorsements of our vision. Mick Power AM, known for his philanthropy and support for educational initiatives, resonated with our goal of creating a vibrant cultural and educational hub. His contribution was instrumental in laying the foundation of the project.

Similarly, with their long-standing commitment to supporting community-driven projects, the John T Reid Charitable Trusts saw the potential impact of a state-of-the-art music centre. Their generosity was a testament to their belief in the power of music education to enrich lives and communities.

These significant contributions were milestones in our journey, ensuring that the music centre's dream would be realised and thrive. The participation of these esteemed donors also acted as a spark, encouraging additional contributions and support from the community, fostering a collective sense of commitment and investment in the future of music education.

Assembling the right team

Central to the success of this ambitious project was the meticulous assembly of a team of experts, each crucial in their respective fields. This team included skilled architects tasked with designing a space that was both aesthetically pleasing and acoustically sound. Acoustical engineers were brought on board to ensure that every note played in the concert hall would resonate perfectly, providing an optimal auditory experience.

Music educators, with their wealth of knowledge and passion for teaching, were integral in shaping the curriculum and the overall educational direction of the music centre. Their expertise was essential in creating a program that would not only educate but also inspire our students.

Administrative staff, proficient in their organisational and operational roles, ensured the smooth running of the centre, dealing with logistics, scheduling, and the myriad details that keep such a facility functioning effectively.

Crucially, the lynchpin of this team was my head of development, Jeff, whom I often called my "partner in crime". Jeff was not just an administrator but a visionary who shared my passion for music education and my ambition for the project. His role transcended typical administrative duties; he was instrumental in networking, fundraising, and bridging the gap between our ambitious goals and their actualisation. His ability to connect with stakeholders, understand the intricacies of the project, and drive it forward with relentless enthusiasm and strategic insight was invaluable.

Together, this diverse and talented team transformed the vision of a world-class music centre and concert hall into a reality, each member playing a vital role in creating a facility that would nurture and showcase musical talent for years to come.

Effective communication and stakeholder engagement

Keeping all stakeholders informed and engaged was a priority. Regular updates, community meetings, and open discussions were instrumental in building support and enthusiasm for the project.

Implementation and adaptation

With the planning phase complete, the implementation began. This stage required close monitoring and the ability to adapt to unexpected challenges, whether construction delays or budgetary changes. Periodic review meetings were key in keeping the project on track.

Launching and beyond

The inauguration of the music centre and concert hall was a beginning, not an end. I oversaw the music program's growth, ensuring high teaching and performance standards. Monitoring our students' progress and the program's impact was essential for ongoing development.

Celebrating success and future planning

As our students achieved remarkable success, celebrating these milestones was important. It not only boosted morale but also showcased the real-world impact of our efforts. Looking forward, plans were made to ensure the sustainability and continued evolution of the music program.

Implementing this transformative change required visionary leadership, meticulous planning, strategic resource management, and a deep commitment to musical excellence. The music centre and concert hall stand as a testament to what can be achieved with a clear vision, a dedicated team, and a passion for enriching lives through music.

4.8 The Fogarty EDvance program

I have chosen this example as a case study on managing change in schools, particularly focusing on closing the education attainment gap in socially disadvantaged communities in Western Australia.

This case study offers several actionable insights and lessons for the reader:

- **Developing a framework based on research and high-performing schools.** The Fogarty EDvance program drew on research and studies of high-performing schools to develop a framework that significantly improved school performance. This approach ensured that the

strategies were grounded in proven methods and tailored to the specific needs of the schools involved.
- **Principles for transformation.** The program emphasised key principles for transforming schools. These included positioning school leaders to oversee and facilitate effective teaching, recognising that each school's path to improvement should be unique, and understanding that sustainable change takes time. Including well-regarded ex-principals as mentors for school leadership teams further supported these principles.
- **Strategic planning and implementation.** The program began by assembling a cohort of schools and creating a strategic plan for each, based on past performance and stakeholder experiences. The second year focused on implementing these plans, including staff upskilling and tracking progress. Emphasis was placed on organisational health, supporting teachers, and maintaining high levels of support.
- **Continuous improvement and sustainability.** The third year involved continuing implementation and tracking, with school leaders creating another three-year plan based on the previous years' work. This ongoing process focused on embedding effective practices and improving performance beyond the program's initial timeframe, highlighting the importance of long-term planning and continuous improvement.

The schools that successfully improved their performance followed several key strategies:

1. Allotting enough time for transformation stages
2. Involving the entire school in the project
3. Developing a common language for understanding and communicating about the transformation
4. Using quantifiable metrics unique to each school
5. Focusing on organisational health, which included clear direction
6. Transparent performance results
7. Support for innovative teaching
8. Leadership continuity
9. A focus on high-impact practices.

These insights from the Fogarty EDvance program illustrate the importance of a well-researched, tailored approach to change management in education, the critical role of leadership and stakeholder involvement, and the need for continuous assessment and adaptation for sustainable improvement (Fogarty EDvance, 2024).

4.9 Key takeaways

As we conclude this chapter on effective change management and innovation in education, several key elements emerge. First, understanding the nature of change is foundational. Recognising the drivers of change, from societal shifts to technological advancements, allows educational leaders to anticipate and prepare proactively.

- **Effective leadership is paramount.** Leaders must set clear visions, motivate staff, and steer strategic directions, especially when navigating complex changes like implementing new programs or building state-of-the-art facilities.
- **Engaging stakeholders**, particularly teachers, in the change process is crucial. Overcoming resistance through empathy, communication, and involvement ensures a more inclusive and effective transformation.
- **Implementing change successfully** requires a meticulous approach, from planning to execution. As seen in ambitious projects like developing specialised facilities, allocating resources, setting timelines, and assembling the right team are critical steps.
- **Continuous improvement and sustainability** are essential for long-term success. Learning from real-world case studies, such as the Fogarty EDvance program, demonstrates the importance of adaptable, research-based strategies and a focus on organisational health.

In summary, navigating the seas of change in education demands adaptability, proactive leadership, and a commitment to continuous growth and improvement. These elements form the bedrock of thriving educational environments that are equipped to face the challenges and opportunities of the future.

CHAPTER 5

MANAGING THE BOARD

5.1 Understanding board dynamics

Managing the school board stands as one of the most pivotal and, indeed, challenging aspects of a principal's role. It is a complex dance of personalities, roles, and power dynamics that, if not navigated astutely, can lead to stress and misalignment in organisational goals. Despite the reluctance of many consultants and board members to embrace this concept, the reality is that principals must effectively "manage" the board to foster a harmonious and productive relationship. It is not about wielding control but about understanding, influencing, and collaborating effectively.

At the heart of board dynamics lies a complex interplay of personalities – each member brings their own beliefs, experiences, and motivations to the table. Some are visionary, always gazing towards the future, while others are guardians of tradition, ensuring the school's heritage remains intact. There are the financial pragmatists, ever watchful of the bottom line, and the educational idealists, who champion pedagogical excellence. Navigating these personalities requires a blend of diplomatic savvy and strategic finesse. It involves recognising each member's strengths and motivations and finding ways to harness these for the collective good of the school.

The roles within a board further add layers to this dynamic. The chair, often seen as the bridge between the board and the principal, is crucial in setting the tone for interactions. Then there are committee chairs and members, each overseeing specific aspects of the school's operations, from finance to risk. Understanding these roles and the responsibilities that come with them is key to effective board management. It's about knowing who to approach on specific issues and how to communicate effectively with each member based on their role and expertise.

Interactions within the board can range from harmonious to contentious, and it is in these interactions that a principal's skills in managing board dynamics are truly tested. It requires active listening, the ability to present ideas persuasively, and, importantly, the skill to build consensus among diverse viewpoints. The principal needs to be a facilitator, a mediator, and sometimes, a negotiator, ensuring that discussions lead to productive outcomes.

At Elmswood Academy (name changed to protect the identity of the school), a storm was brewing that threatened to disrupt the harmonious leadership that had long guided its halls. When Jonathan Harris (not his true name), a parent with a charismatic presence and a persuasive voice, was elected to the school board, it seemed like a promising addition. However, it soon became evident that his intentions were far from benign. Harris had an agenda that was meticulously crafted to undermine my leadership as the principal. Initially, his tactics were subtle but they grew increasingly aggressive, aiming to drive a wedge between me and the other board members. Once a haven for constructive dialogue and collaborative decision-making, board meetings became battlegrounds, with Harris orchestrating a campaign of discord.

The situation reached a critical point when Harris's actions began to affect the school's overall atmosphere. The board, initially patient and willing to entertain Harris's perspectives, grew weary of his divisive tactics. It became clear that his presence was more than just a challenge to my leadership; it was a threat to the school's core values of unity and constructive collaboration. In a decisive move, the board members united to safeguard their school's ethos. Harris's term was terminated, sending a clear message that caustic and divisive behaviours had no place in the governance of Elmswood Academy. This bold action by the board not only reinstated harmony but also reinforced the foundational principles that the school stood for.

Key lessons for boards from this case study

1. **Vigilance in board member selection.** Boards must exercise due diligence in evaluating the intentions and background of potential members to ensure alignment with the school's values and leadership.
2. **Unity and solidarity.** It is crucial for board members to maintain a united front, especially in the face of attempts to sow discord.

Solidarity among board members can act as a strong deterrent against divisive tactics.
3. **Upholding institutional values.** Boards should always prioritise the core values and ethos of the institution. Any member who consistently acts in contradiction of these values might not be a suitable fit for the board.
4. **Effective conflict resolution.** Boards need to develop strategies for early identification and resolution of conflicts. This includes having clear policies on handling situations where a board member's actions are detrimental to the school's leadership and harmony.
5. **Transparency and communication.** Maintaining open lines of communication within the board and with the school leadership is key. This ensures that any underlying issues are addressed promptly and transparently.

In summary, managing the board is not about subverting its authority but about guiding it towards effective governance. It is about building a relationship based on mutual respect, shared goals, and clear communication. When a principal understands and adeptly manages these dynamics, the board becomes not just a governing body but a powerful ally in achieving the school's vision.

This chapter sets the stage for a deeper exploration of the skills required to manage school boards – a journey that's as challenging as it is rewarding and can significantly impact a school's success.

5.2 Effective communication strategies

Effective communication with board members is a cornerstone of successful school leadership. It is a skill that transcends mere transmission of information; it involves strategic presentation, active listening, and facilitating meaningful discussions. The board report emerges as a pivotal tool in this intricate dance, offering a structured platform for information-sharing and decision-making. However, communication with board members outside of official meetings and reports requires careful consideration and is generally reserved for exceptional circumstances.

The board report. This is a principal's tool for presenting data, achievements, challenges, and strategies in a clear and concise manner. When preparing your board report, prioritise relevance and clarity. Start with an executive summary that highlights the main points and the decisions that need to be made. Continue with detailed sections covering different aspects of school operations – finance, academics, student welfare, staff development, and strategic initiatives. Use data effectively to substantiate your points, but be careful not to overwhelm the members with too much information. The goal of the report is to inform and engage the board, encouraging their active participation in the school's progress.

Active listening and feedback. Effective communication is a two-way street. During board meetings, practise active listening. Show genuine interest in members' viewpoints, acknowledge their concerns, and seek clarification when needed. Encouraging open dialogue fosters a sense of collaboration. When receiving feedback, whether positive or critical, accept it graciously. Use it as a learning opportunity and a means to build trust and rapport with the board.

Facilitating productive discussions. As a principal, you are crucial in steering board discussions. Frame agenda items clearly, provide necessary background information, and be prepared to answer questions. Keep discussions focused and on track, but allow room for creative and critical thinking. When disagreements arise, mediate diplomatically to find common ground or a viable compromise.

Communicating outside board meetings. While the norm is to communicate with the board collectively and within the formal structures of meetings and reports, there are occasions when direct communication outside these channels is necessary. Such instances include:

- **Emergency situations.** In case of a crisis or emergency that significantly impacts the school (e.g., natural disasters, critical security incidents), immediate communication with the board is imperative.
- **Legal and compliance issues.** If there are urgent legal or compliance matters that require immediate attention or pose significant risk to the school, the board should be informed promptly.
- **Significant financial concerns.** Urgent financial issues that could have major implications for the school's operations or reputation warrant immediate board notification.
- **Reputational matters.** If an event occurs that could significantly impact the school's reputation (e.g., a major public relations issue), it is prudent to inform the board as soon as possible.
- **Personnel issues.** Situations involving senior staff, such as sudden resignations or serious misconduct, may necessitate direct communication with the board.

In all such communications, maintain professionalism and discretion. The goal is to keep the board adequately informed without circumventing the established protocols of collective decision-making. Remember, the exceptional nature of these communications should not undermine the principles of structured and collaborative governance.

The board chair. Effective communication with the board chair is a nuanced aspect of a principal's role, integral to the smooth operation and governance of the school. This relationship should be marked by regular, open dialogue and mutual respect. The board chair acts as a key liaison between the principal and the rest of the board, making it essential to keep them informed on all major school developments, challenges, and successes.

Communication with the chair should be forthright yet tactful, ensuring they are the first to know about any significant issues or changes within the school. This ongoing dialogue helps pre-empt misunderstandings, align strategic visions, and ensure that the board and the school leadership work cohesively towards common goals. It's a partnership that requires honesty, trust, and regular engagement to effectively navigate the complexities of school governance.

Case study - the rogue board director's gambit

At one of my schools, a respected school known for its collaborative leadership and dedicated staff, an unforeseen challenge emerged that tested its governance. A board director, dissatisfied with my action plan regarding a new curriculum integration across the senior school, decided to take matters into her own hands. Disregarding the established protocols and the sanctity of board conduct, she began an unauthorised inquiry into my performance. She bypassed the traditional communication channels and directly approached a small number of school staff, soliciting unstructured and informal feedback. This move, motivated by her disagreement with my approach, soon turned into a witch hunt, as the board director sought ammunition to challenge me in upcoming board meetings. Her actions not only breached board conduct but also created an atmosphere of distrust and unease among the staff, who were caught off guard by her direct inquiries.

This situation escalated to a point where it not only questioned the board director's adherence to board ethics but also threatened stability and morale within the school. Feeling undermined and confused, the staff found themselves in a difficult position, torn between their loyalty to me and the pressure exerted by a board member. Upon becoming aware of her actions, the board faced a critical decision: how to address this breach of conduct and restore the balance of trust and authority that is essential for the effective operation of the school. To exacerbate the problem, some of her colleagues on the board were complicit in the breaches by allowing her to go unchecked.

Insights – proper conduct for board directors

1. **Adherence to protocols.** Board directors should strictly adhere to established communication protocols. If a director has concerns about any aspect of the school's operations, these should be addressed through formal channels, such as scheduled board meetings or designated committees.
2. **Respect for roles and boundaries.** It is crucial for board members to respect the boundaries of their roles. Direct communication with staff about management issues can create conflict and confusion and undermine the authority of the school leadership.
3. **Constructive engagement.** If a board member disagrees with a specific action plan or decision, they should engage constructively by presenting their concerns and alternative solutions during board discussions. This fosters a collaborative approach to problem-solving.
4. **Seeking formal evaluation methods.** Instead of soliciting informal feedback from staff, board members should rely on structured and formal performance evaluation processes that are fair, transparent, and agreed upon by the board and school leadership.
5. **Maintaining professionalism and confidentiality.** Board directors must maintain high professionalism and confidentiality. Personal disagreements should not translate into actions that disrupt the school's functioning or its leadership.

By understanding and adhering to these principles, board members can contribute positively to the governance of the school, ensuring that their actions benefit the school community as a whole.

In conclusion, mastering effective communication with the board is about balancing the formality of structured reports and meetings with the agility to respond to exceptional circumstances. It is about building a relationship based on transparency, respect, and mutual understanding, which ultimately leads to effective governance and the successful stewardship of the school.

5.3 Building and maintaining trust

In the important relationship between a school board and its leadership, trust is the bedrock upon which effective governance is built. This trust is not merely a feel-good factor but an operational imperative. It enables smooth decision-making, effective communication, and the alignment of goals between the board and the school leadership. However, building and maintaining this trust requires a deliberate and consistent approach.

Strategies for building trust

- **Transparency in communication.** Be open and honest in your communications with the board. Share both successes and challenges. Transparency breeds trust by demonstrating that you have nothing to hide and are committed to the school's best interests.
- **Consistency and reliability.** Demonstrate consistency in your actions and decisions. Reliability in fulfilling commitments and following through on promises is crucial in building trust.
- **Informed decision-making.** Base your decisions on well-researched and analysed data. Presenting well-thought-out plans and strategies to the board shows you are a competent and thoughtful leader.
- **Active listening and empathy.** Show genuine interest in board members' opinions and concerns. Understanding their perspectives and addressing their concerns where possible creates mutual respect that is foundational to trust.
- **Shared vision and goals.** Work with the board to develop and agree on a shared vision and set of goals for the school. Aligning your leadership with these objectives demonstrates your commitment to the collective mission.
- **Regular and structured updates.** Keep the board regularly informed about school operations, student achievements, and other important matters. Regular updates prevent surprises and help the board feel involved and informed.

Avoiding damage to trust

While building trust is a process, damaging it can occur swiftly and often inadvertently. Here are some pitfalls to avoid:

- **Withholding information.** Deliberately withholding information, especially that which is critical or potentially controversial,

- can be detrimental to trust. It suggests a lack of integrity or fear of accountability.
- **Inconsistency.** Frequent changes in positions, policies, or promises can erode trust. Consistency is key in demonstrating stability and reliability.
- **Defensiveness or avoidance.** Being defensive in the face of critique or avoiding difficult conversations can signal a lack of confidence or transparency.
- **Overpromising and underdelivering.** Avoid making commitments you cannot keep. Setting realistic expectations is better than failing to meet overly ambitious ones.
- **Ignoring board input.** Regularly disregarding the advice or input of board members can breed resentment and mistrust. While you may not always agree, it is important to consider their perspectives seriously.

Trust between the board and school leadership is a critical element that requires careful cultivation and nurturing. It's about more than just getting along; it is about building a partnership based on mutual respect, shared goals, and open communication. Maintaining this trust involves consistent and honest interactions, as well as a keen awareness of the actions and attitudes that can undermine it.

Case study – toxic influences undermined faith and confidence in the principal

In the often-complex landscape of principalship, a cautionary tale serves as a reminder of the delicate nature of trust within the dynamics of school governance. This story revolves around a principal, well-respected for their competence and commitment, who found themselves ensnared in a web of mistrust not of their own making.

Despite years of high performance and experience, this principal became the unintended target of a toxic campaign led by a group of parents. Unfounded and vicious rumours began to spread, creating an atmosphere of doubt and suspicion. In an effort to uphold integrity, the principal tackled these rumours head-on, addressing them with openness and honesty, but the tide of misinformation proved too strong.

The situation escalated as the board chair became personally involved in the matter. The chair would have remained impartial in an ideal world, facilitating a fair and objective investigation. However, in this case, their personal entanglement skewed the board's perspective, transforming the issue into a divisive stand-off: support the chair or stand by the principal.

Regrettably, the board made a choice that would have lasting repercussions. They sided with their chair, a decision that, while perhaps aligned with their personal loyalties, overlooked the absence of evidence against the principal. This decision, driven more by internal politics than factual accuracy, led to an unfortunate and undeserved outcome for the principal.

The rumours, baseless as they were, managed to tarnish a career built on years of dedication and success. The principal, caught in a maelstrom of untruths, faced the harsh reality of a damaged reputation and a derailed professional journey.

This narrative serves as a stark reminder of the fragility of trust and the devastating impact of rumours and misinformation. It underscores the importance of unbiased, transparent decision-making processes within school boards and the dire consequences when these are compromised. Ultimately, it is a story highlighting the need for principled leadership, not just in school administration but also at the board level, where the balance of support and scrutiny must be navigated with fairness and integrity.

Lessons learned

In the case study described, the principal faced a challenging situation due to toxic influences and a lack of support from the board. However, there are strategies the principal could have employed to possibly rescue or at least mitigate the situation.

1. **Engage in proactive communication.** The principal could have taken a more proactive approach in communicating with all stakeholders, including parents, staff, and board members. This would have involved organising meetings or forums to openly discuss the issues, address any misconceptions, and provide clarity on their actions and decisions. Transparent and frequent communication might have helped in countering misinformation and rebuilding trust.

2. **Seek external mediation or support.** Given the complexity of the situation, especially with the board chair's involvement, the principal could have sought external mediation or advice. This could have been from an educational consultant, a legal advisor, or a professional mediator. An unbiased third party might have helped in facilitating discussions between the principal, the board, and the concerned parents, aiming to find a mutually acceptable resolution.

3. **Document and present evidence of performance.** To counter the baseless rumours and reinforce their professional credibility, the principal could have compiled and presented comprehensive evidence of their performance and contributions to the school. This documentation could have included success stories, improvements in school performance, positive feedback from staff and parents, and any awards or recognitions received. Presenting this evidence to the board, or even the wider school community, could have helped demonstrate the principal's competence and dedication, potentially swaying opinions in their favour.

These strategies are not guaranteed solutions but represent proactive steps a leader might take in such a complex and challenging scenario. It is crucial for principals to maintain open lines of communication, seek support when needed, and continually document their performance and achievements as part of their leadership strategy.

5.4 Strategic planning and goal setting – principal-led collaboration with the board

The process of strategic planning and goal setting is pivotal. The crux of this discourse is not about who steers the ship but rather how effectively the journey is navigated. While some consultants, particularly those from the governor's camp, may argue for a board-led approach, a compelling case exists for the principal, in tandem with the executive team, to take the helm in this endeavour.

The principal's edge – understanding and context

The principal and the executive team are the architects of the school's daily operations. They possess a nuanced understanding of the school's context, its unique challenges and potential opportunities. This profound knowledge base enables them to set realistic and achievable goals that resonate with the learners' needs and the institution's educational ethos.

Knowledge of the terrain. The principal and their team are entrenched in the educational environment. They understand the learners' needs, the teachers' capabilities, and the school's resources. This intimate knowledge is critical in crafting goals that are aspirational and grounded in the reality of the school's capabilities and limitations.

Appreciation of challenges and opportunities. School leadership is adept at navigating the complex landscape of educational challenges and leveraging opportunities. Whether integrating technology in classrooms, adopting new pedagogical strategies, or addressing socio-economic disparities among students, the executive team is best positioned to identify and prioritise these aspects in goal setting.

The role of the board – strategic involvement

While not directly involved in day-to-day operations, the school board plays a crucial role in the broader strategic framework. Their involvement is vital in ensuring that the goals set by the principal and the executive team align with broader educational objectives and policy directions. The board's strategic oversight and governance expertise complement the operational leadership of the school's executive team.

Collaborative dynamics. Effective collaboration between the principal and the board is essential. The principal should lead the goal-setting process, leveraging the board's insights for strategic alignment. This synergy ensures the goals are ambitious yet attainable, innovative yet in line with broader educational policies.

Mutual respect and understanding. There must be mutual respect and understanding for this collaboration to be fruitful. The board should recognise the principal's expertise in educational leadership, while the principal should value the board's strategic perspective. This reciprocal appreciation fosters a constructive environment for setting and achieving goals.

Principal-led, board-supported

In my view, the principal, supported by the executive team, should lead the strategic planning and goal-setting process. Their deep understanding of the school's context and educational expertise uniquely position them for this role. The board's strategic involvement and oversight provide a complementary balance, ensuring the goals align with broader educational objectives. The synergy between the principal and the board is not just desirable but necessary for the successful realisation of the school's vision and mission.

5.5 Navigating conflict and differences of opinion – the case of mishandled parental complaints

Conflict resolution within a school's administrative framework, especially in the context of board-level disputes, is a nuanced and complex task. This subchapter explores how a principal can effectively manage situations where a school board has mishandled a parent's complaint, leading to potential conflict and differences of opinion.

The scenario – a mishandled parental complaint

When a school board inadequately addresses a parent's complaint, it places the principal in a delicate and often stressful situation. The principal's response in these circumstances is critical for their personal well-being and for preserving the integrity and function of the school's operations.

Strategies for effective conflict resolution:

- **Maintain professional composure.** The principal should remain calm and composed, avoiding impulsive reactions that could worsen the situation. A composed demeanour aids in rational decision-making and demonstrates leadership under pressure.
- **Initiate open communication.** Requesting a private meeting with the board is a critical step. This meeting is a platform to discuss the complaint and its handling constructively. The principal should aim to clarify misunderstandings and express concerns diplomatically.
- **Present facts objectively.** In the meeting, it is crucial to present the facts of the complaint clearly and objectively. Avoid assigning blame; focus on the impact of the board's actions on the school's environment and the principal's position.
- **Maintain documentation.** Keeping a detailed record of all interactions and communications related to the complaint is essential. This documentation can provide necessary support and clarity if the issue escalates.
- **Seek support.** The principal should not hesitate to seek advice from mentors, professional networks, or even legal counsel, particularly if the situation affects their mental health or professional standing.
- **Propose constructive solutions.** Rather than dwelling on the mishandling, the principal should suggest practical solutions or request specific support from the board. This could include establishing clearer communication protocols or involving mediation services.
- **Focus on a constructive resolution.** The principal's approach should be geared towards finding a resolution that serves the best interests of all parties involved, including the school, the board, and the concerned parents.

Advocacy and professionalism

In situations where the principal faces conflict due to the board's mishandling of a parent's complaint, their approach can set a precedent for future conflict resolution. The principal can navigate these challenges by maintaining professionalism, advocating for constructive solutions, and focusing on clear communication. This balanced approach addresses the immediate issue and strengthens the principal's position as a leader capable of handling complex administrative challenges.

5.6 Specific models to consider for handling disputes

The Dispute System Design (Arnold, 1995)

In addressing the complexities of handling conflicts and complaints in schools, adopting a Dispute System Design (DSD) can be instrumental. DSD is an overarching framework that encompasses various methods for managing disputes, including complaints, mediations, and conflict resolution processes. For schools, developing a robust DSD involves creating policies and procedures that are clear, consistent, and collaboratively formed with input from all relevant stakeholders – teachers, administrators, parents, and possibly students.

An effective DSD ensures that every step of the conflict resolution process is transparent and accessible, which helps not only in managing disputes when they arise but also in preventing many conflicts from escalating. Key components of a school's DSD might include designated personnel for conflict resolution, standardised procedures for filing and addressing complaints, and regular training sessions for staff on effective dispute resolution techniques. Schools need to invest in these systems to enhance their capability to manage conflicts efficiently and maintain a harmonious educational environment.

The CIV Approach to Conflict Resolution (Rosenberg, 2015)

When managing differences of opinion, especially in sensitive situations like parental complaints, it is crucial to employ communication strategies that foster understanding without necessarily leading to agreement.

One effective method is the CIV approach, which stands for Connect, Invite, and Validate. Initially, "connect" with the individual by engaging in a conversation on a neutral topic to build rapport. Following this, "invite"' them to share their perspective on the conflict, listening attentively to their concerns. Finally, "validate" their feelings and viewpoints, acknowledging the significance of the issue from their perspective.

This method does not require that parties agree but ensures that each feels heard and understood, which can significantly defuse tension and pave the way for constructive dialogue. Integrating the CIV approach into a school's dispute resolution policy can greatly enhance the effectiveness of its conflict management, ensuring that disputes are handled with empathy and respect, thereby maintaining trust and positive relationships within the school community.

5.7 Crucial relationships

The relationship between the principal and the CFO/bursar/business manager

In some long-established schools, the business manager reports directly to the board and not to the principal. I do not advocate that model for schools. The business manager must be accountable to the principal and be a direct report to the principal. It is reasonable for the business manager to provide financial reports to the school board's finance committee, but the lines of accountability must be clear to the principal. This structure ensures that financial strategies are closely aligned with the school's educational objectives and day-to-day operations.

The relationship between the school principal and the CFO/bursar/business manager is fundamental to the success of any school. This partnership must be built on a foundation of mutual trust and clear communication, as virtually every decision made within the school has financial implications. A strong, collaborative relationship ensures that the school's vision is financially viable and sustainable. Therefore, while all stakeholders play significant roles, the business manager indeed holds a special place in the school's governance structure.

Together, the principal and business manager strategise to align financial resources with educational goals, ensuring that the school not only achieves its vision but does so within a sustainable financial framework. Maintaining this reporting structure not only clarifies responsibilities but also strengthens the governance needed to support the school's strategic directions.

Key conflict points in relationships with the board

Understanding the common conflict points, such as power/control, trust, and respect/recognition, is crucial in managing relationships with the board and its chair. These elements are often at the core of challenges faced by school leaders, particularly in the dynamics between the principal and the chair of the board. The relationship between the principal and the chair is pivotal, as it sets the tone for the entire board's interaction with school management and can significantly influence the school's strategic direction.

To enhance the effectiveness of board management and mitigate potential conflicts, it is essential for the principal and chair to establish a robust partnership based on mutual respect and open communication. This relationship should be characterised by regular, structured dialogues where both parties feel comfortable discussing and debating school policies and strategies openly. Such interactions help prevent misunderstandings and ensure that decisions are made collaboratively, reflecting both the educational expertise of the principal and the governance acumen of the chair.

Moreover, the principal and chair should work together to foster a culture of transparency and accountability within the board. This can be achieved by jointly developing clear decision-making protocols and ensuring that these are adhered to consistently. By demonstrating a united front, they can set an example for how conflicts should be handled constructively, thereby fostering an atmosphere where trust thrives.

Recognising and valuing the contributions of each board member is also critical. The principal and chair can lead by example, ensuring that all members feel their voices are heard and that their contributions are recognised. This not only bolsters respect and recognition across the board but also enhances member engagement and commitment to the school's mission.

In conclusion, the relationship between the principal and the chair is not merely administrative; it is the cornerstone of effective school governance. By prioritising this relationship, schools can ensure smoother navigation through the challenges of board management, ultimately leading to a governance structure that robustly supports the school's strategic objectives and enhances its educational impact.

Operational vs strategic management

The division of responsibilities between operational management, typically within the purview of the principal, and strategic oversight, shared between the board and the principal, provides a fundamental framework for school governance. However, this distinction, while helpful, might sometimes oversimplify the complexities of managing a school. Operational decisions, though primarily the responsibility of the principal, often carry strategic implications that can influence the school's broader objectives, and strategic decisions made by the board can significantly impact daily operations.

To maintain a healthy balance and prevent the board from stepping into management roles that should rightly belong to the principal, it is crucial to establish clear boundaries and communication protocols. The principal, acting as the CEO of the school, must be afforded the autonomy to manage day-to-day operations and make operational decisions that align with the school's established strategic framework. This autonomy is essential not only for effective management but also for empowering the principal to act swiftly and decisively in response to immediate operational needs.

Conversely, the principal's monthly report to the board plays a vital role in maintaining this balance. By systematically informing the board of key operational developments, significant achievements, and challenges, the principal ensures that the board remains adequately informed without needing to step into the management arena. This report should highlight matters of strategic importance, providing the board with insight into how operational decisions are supporting the school's long-term strategic goals.

Furthermore, adopting a more integrated approach where strategic and operational decisions are discussed collaboratively can lead to more cohesive and effective management. Regular strategic meetings and retreats involving both the principal and the board can facilitate this integration, ensuring that while the principal manages the day-to-day operations, the strategic vision guided by the board aligns seamlessly with these activities. This not only enhances the school's ability to achieve its long-term goals but also fosters a sense of shared purpose and mutual respect between the board and the management.

In summary, while the principal should operate with considerable autonomy in managing the school, a structured approach to strategic alignment and communication with the board is essential. This framework helps prevent overreach by the board into operational matters and ensures that both the board and the principal work in concert to navigate the complexities of school management effectively, ultimately enhancing the educational environment for all stakeholders.

5.8 Your time is up, and you didn't see it coming

It is crucial to address the reality that principals may face unexpected non-renewal of their contracts.

For principals, especially those nearing the end of a multi-year contract, the possibility of non-renewal can be a blindsiding and career-altering event. To mitigate this risk, it is essential to proactively engage in strategies that ensure alignment with the board's expectations and the evolving needs of the school.

Regular and transparent communication with the board is key. Principals should seek to understand the board's long-term vision and objectives and align their goals and strategies accordingly. Regular performance discussions and feedback sessions with the board can provide insights into their perceptions and any areas of concern.

Principals should also actively engage in self-evaluation and professional development. Staying updated with educational trends and leadership strategies, and reflecting on one's own performance, can help in adapting to changing demands and expectations.

Building a strong leadership team and fostering a positive school culture are equally important. Demonstrating effective leadership and positive outcomes can reinforce the principal's value to the school.

Lastly, networking and maintaining professional relationships outside the current school environment can provide alternative opportunities and insights. This broader perspective can offer warning signs or confirmations about the principal's standing and future prospects.

By staying proactive, engaged, and adaptable, principals can better position themselves to either secure contract renewal or gracefully transition to new opportunities should the unexpected occur.

5.9 Legal and ethical considerations

Cautionary tale – the perils of rogue lawyers and litigation

In legal and ethical considerations, there exists a notable hazard: rogue lawyers who prioritise litigation over client care. This highlights the critical need for vigilance and discernment in the selection and management of legal counsel.

Some lawyers, driven by personal motives or a predisposition towards confrontational tactics, may push for litigation as the first course of action. This aggressive approach often overlooks the nuances of client care, particularly in the sensitive context of educational environments. Litigation can escalate conflicts, strain relationships, and create an adversarial atmosphere, which is antithetical to the collaborative and community-focused ethos of a school.

Case study – litigation without foresight

Consider a scenario where a school board, influenced by a litigious lawyer, opts to take a parental complaint to court without thoroughly exploring alternative dispute resolution methods. The legal process becomes protracted, draining the school's resources – both financially and in terms of staff morale. The community's trust in the school is eroded, and the legal outcome, irrespective of its favourability, leaves a lasting scar on the school's reputation.

This situation exemplifies the pitfalls of engaging with lawyers who favour court battles over more amicable and constructive solutions. It highlights the need for the risk and compliance subcommittee to carefully vet legal counsel and ensure their approach aligns with the school's values and long-term interests.

The principal's role in mitigating legal risks

In collaboration with the risk and compliance subcommittee, the principal should advocate for a balanced and thoughtful approach to legal challenges. It involves:

- **Assessing legal counsel.** Diligently evaluate the track record and approach of legal advisors. Ensure their methods align with the school's ethos and prioritise the well-being of the school community.
- **Promoting alternative dispute resolution.** Encourage methods like mediation or arbitration as first-line strategies. These approaches often lead to more amicable solutions and preserve important community relationships.

- **Educating the board.** The principal, aided by the subcommittee, should educate board members about the potential consequences of aggressive legal tactics. This awareness can guide the board towards making more informed and considered decisions.

Prudence over pugnacity

While legal counsel is indispensable, engaging with lawyers who understand the unique context of schools and prioritising the school's long-term well-being over short-term legal victories is crucial. The principal, alongside the risk and compliance subcommittee, plays a pivotal role in steering the school clear of unnecessary legal battles and fostering an environment where legal and ethical considerations are balanced with client care and community values.

The governance of schools encompasses a broad spectrum of legal and ethical responsibilities. A critical role is played by the board risk and compliance subcommittee, particularly one that includes a member with legal expertise. This structure is essential in guiding the board through complex legal landscapes and ensuring adherence to ethical standards in decision-making processes. The principal's role in this setup, complemented by access to legal advice, is a pivotal aspect of navigating the increasingly complex demands of educational leadership.

The role of the risk and compliance subcommittee

- **Legal expertise on the board.** The presence of a board member with legal experience is invaluable. They bring a deep understanding of legal intricacies that can influence board decisions. Their expertise ensures that the board's actions are legally sound and ethically aligned.
- **Monitoring legal compliance.** This subcommittee is tasked with keeping abreast of laws and regulations that impact the school. It ensures that the board's decisions comply with these legal frameworks, thereby mitigating risks and upholding the school's integrity.
- **Ethical decision-making.** Ethical considerations are as crucial as legal ones. The subcommittee guides the board in maintaining ethical standards, ensuring decisions reflect the school's values and community expectations.

The principal's interaction with the subcommittee

- **Strategic legal guidance.** The principal benefits immensely from having direct access to legal advice. A board member with legal

expertise can offer practical, no-nonsense advice to the principal, especially in dealing with complex issues such as parental complaints or contractual matters.
- **Proactive approach to legal challenges.** The principal, equipped with legal insights, can proactively address potential legal issues before they escalate. This foresight can be instrumental in avoiding legal pitfalls and maintaining the school's reputation.
- **Navigating "bush lawyer" parent syndrome.** In an era where parents are increasingly well-informed (and sometimes misinformed) about legal matters, the principal can leverage legal advice to address and clarify such issues confidently and authoritatively.

Ensuring access to legal counsel

1. **Incorporating legal advice in decision-making.** The principal should integrate legal counsel into the decision-making process, particularly for decisions with significant legal implications.
2. **Cost-effective legal support.** While budget constraints are a reality, the value of having legal advice "in the principal's hip pocket" cannot be overstated. The board should prioritise this as a necessary investment, recognising its potential to save costs and legal hassles in the long run.

Legal and ethical vigilance as a cornerstone

The establishment of a risk and compliance subcommittee, particularly one with legal expertise, is not just a recommendation but a necessity in the modern educational landscape. It equips the board and the principal with the necessary tools to navigate legal and ethical complexities confidently. Access to legal counsel is a critical asset for the principal, enabling them to address issues with authority and foresight. This approach not only safeguards the school legally but also reinforces its commitment to ethical governance.

5.10 Key takeaways

As we conclude this chapter, it is vital to distil the key insights and strategies that have been discussed. This final subchapter synthesises the essential takeaways, offering educational leaders a clear guide to effectively working with and managing school boards.

1. **Understanding the board's perspective**

    Insight: Recognising board members' motivations, priorities, and concerns is fundamental.

Application: Engage in regular, open dialogue with board members to understand their viewpoints and expectations.

2. **Effective communication and transparency**

    Insight: Clear and honest communication forms the backbone of a strong relationship with the board.

    Application: Keep the board informed about school developments and decisions and ensure transparency in all communications.

3. **Strategic alignment and goal setting**

    Insight: Aligning the school's strategic goals with the board's vision is crucial.

    Application: Collaboratively work with the board to set realistic and achievable goals, ensuring they align with broader educational objectives.

4. **Navigating conflicts and differences**

    Insight: Conflicts and differences of opinion are inevitable but manageable through effective strategies.
    Application: Employ conflict resolution techniques and seek common ground or compromise when needed.

5. **Legal and ethical considerations**

    Insight: Adhering to legal and ethical standards is non-negotiable in board management.

    Application: Ensure a risk and compliance subcommittee, ideally with legal expertise, is in place to guide decision-making processes.

6. **Building collaborative relationships**

    Insight: A collaborative approach with the board fosters mutual respect and effective governance.

    Application: Involve the board meaningfully, valuing their input and expertise.

7. **Professional development and support**

    Insight: Continual learning and professional support are essential for navigating board dynamics.

    Application: Seek mentorship, join professional networks, and engage in ongoing education about effective board management.

The Australian Institute of Company Directors is a rich resource for principals (as CEOs) wanting to build their governance acumen. I found a great mentor in a very experienced (current at the time) and late-career principal; we would catch up for a game of golf routinely to "chew the fat" about board dynamics.

In managing the board, it is essential to balance professionalism, strategic thinking, and effective communication. The relationship between the principal and the board is pivotal to the school's success. By embracing these key takeaways, educational leaders can forge a positive and productive partnership with their boards, navigating challenges and capitalising on opportunities for the betterment of their educational institutions.

CHAPTER 6

MANAGING STICKY SITUATIONS AND STAKEHOLDERS

6.1 Untangling complex webs

Education is not just about pedagogy and learning; it is also an intricate web of relationships and interests, where various stakeholders often have competing priorities and perspectives. This chapter examines the strategies and insights necessary for handling challenging stakeholder dynamics, an essential skill for any educational leader.

Ultimately, the goal is to build a harmonious educational community where each stakeholder feels heard and valued. This chapter equips school leaders with the tools and knowledge to manage stakeholder relationships proactively, ensuring that even the most challenging situations are handled with tact, empathy, and strategic foresight.

At the outset, it's important to recognise the diverse array of stakeholders that a school leader interacts with: students, parents, teachers, administrative staff, board members, and community representatives, among others. Each group has its distinct set of expectations and influence, shaping the decisions and policies of a school. Navigating these relationships requires a deep understanding of the stakeholders' needs and motivations, and the power they wield within the educational ecosystem.

The core of this chapter focuses on strategies to manage these complex relationships effectively. It involves identifying the most challenging stakeholders, understanding their concerns, and finding ways to engage with them constructively.

Balancing diverse needs and expectations

A significant challenge in managing tricky stakeholders is balancing different groups' diverse needs and expectations while staying true to the school's vision and goals. This balancing act requires diplomatic skills and a clear understanding of the school's strategic objectives. It is about finding common ground, building consensus, and sometimes making tough decisions that may only please some but serve the greater good of the educational community.

When selecting an independent school in Australia, parents consider various factors to ensure the best fit for their child's education and well-being:

1. **Academic reputation and performance.** Parents often prioritise schools with a strong academic track record, including HSC results (in the NSW context, for example), NAPLAN results, a history of students being accepted into prestigious universities, and a curriculum that challenges and engages students.
2. **Specialised programs.** Independent schools offer specialised programs such as STEM (Science, Technology, Engineering, and Mathematics), arts, sports, or languages. Parents may choose a school that aligns with their child's interests or talents.
3. **Values and philosophy.** The ethos or philosophy of a school, such as religious affiliation, a focus on holistic education, or a particular educational approach (like Montessori or Steiner education), can be a deciding factor for parents who want their child's education to align with family values or beliefs.
4. **Quality of facilities.** State-of-the-art sports, arts, sciences, and technology facilities can be a drawcard. Well-equipped classrooms, libraries, and other learning spaces can greatly enhance the educational experience.
5. **Extracurricular activities.** A wide range of extracurricular activities, including clubs, sports teams, music and arts programs, and overseas trips, can be appealing. These activities are seen as important for the all-round development of a child. Rowing, for example, is a drawcard for some families.

6. **Class size and individual attention.** Smaller class sizes in some independent schools can mean more individual attention for each student, which is often seen as beneficial for academic and personal development. It is one measure parents will use when comparing the benefits of high-fee-paying schools with the lower-fee-paying neighbour "down the road".
7. **Location and accessibility.** Proximity to home or work, ease of transportation, and the safety of the school's location are practical considerations that can heavily influence a parent's choice – for example, if it is close to a train line.

These factors vary in importance from family to family, but they commonly play a significant role in the decision-making process for choosing an independent school in Australia.

Case study – navigating parental concerns at Sunnyside Academy

I have changed the names to protect the identities of the principal and school.

Sunnyside Academy, a well-regarded independent school in Melbourne, Australia, faced a challenge when a group of parents raised concerns about the school's new digital learning initiative. The initiative involved integrating technology more deeply into the curriculum, which the school leadership, including Principal Thompson, believed was crucial for modernising education and preparing students for a digital future.

A vocal group of parents, however, expressed strong reservations. They were concerned about increased screen time, potential distractions, and the loss of traditional teaching methods. As the disagreement escalated, it threatened to divide the school community.

Understanding the gravity of the situation, Principal Thompson tackled the issue head-on through a series of strategic steps. Principal Thompson identified the concerned parents as key stakeholders and sought to understand their perspectives. She organised a series of small group meetings to listen to their concerns, demonstrating empathy and a willingness to engage in open dialogue.

She organised a town hall meeting, providing a platform for open discussion. Here, she presented the rationale behind the digital learning initiative, backed by educational research and examples from other schools that had successfully integrated technology into their curricula.

Recognising the validity of some parental concerns, Principal Thompson proposed a collaborative approach. She formed a committee comprising teachers, parents, and external experts to develop guidelines for the responsible use of technology in the classroom.

Instead of a full-scale roll-out, she proposed a pilot program in select classes, with continuous monitoring and regular feedback sessions. This approach allowed for adjustments to be made in real time, addressing concerns as they arose.

Principal Thompson ensured that the process was transparent and inclusive. Regular updates were provided to the entire school community, and the feedback was taken seriously. This approach helped build trust and demonstrated that the school leadership valued parental input.

The pilot program was successful, with students showing increased engagement and improved learning outcomes. The parents involved in the committee appreciated the balanced approach to technology use. The initiative was eventually implemented school-wide, with guidelines reflecting a consensus among all stakeholders.

Lessons learned
1. Engaging stakeholders directly and empathetically can turn a potential conflict into an opportunity for collaboration.
2. Transparency and open communication are key to building trust.
3. Involving stakeholders in the decision-making process ensures that diverse perspectives are considered, leading to more sustainable solutions.

Anticipating technological advancements and integrating them into educational frameworks is a critical role for any principal. By pioneering the use of artificial intelligence and machine learning in their curriculum, Sunnyside Academy not only stayed ahead of technological trends but also shaped how these technologies were perceived and adopted within the educational sector. This proactive stance enabled their students to be not just consumers but also creators of technology, positioning their school at the forefront of educational innovation.

6.2 Communication in the eye of the storm

In schools, conflicts are inevitable. How a leader communicates during these challenging times can make the difference between escalating and resolving a situation effectively. This subchapter focuses on strategies for maintaining clear and empathetic communication during conflicts, emphasising active listening, composure, and effective message conveyance.

Active listening – the foundation of conflict resolution

Active listening is the foundation of effective conflict management. It involves fully concentrating, understanding, responding, and remembering what is being said. In a dispute, leaders often focus on formulating a response while the other person is still speaking, leading to misunderstandings. Instead, active listening requires patience and an open mind. A leader can build trust and create a foundation for mutual understanding by truly hearing stakeholders' concerns and acknowledging their feelings. This process involves hearing the words and paying attention to non-verbal cues like tone and body language.

Maintaining composure – a leader's anchor

During conflicts, emotions can run high. A leader's ability to maintain composure under pressure is crucial. Composure should not be confused with emotional detachment; rather, it's about remaining calm and respectful, regardless of how heated the situation becomes. This self-regulation ensures that the focus remains on the issue rather than personal feelings. Techniques such as deep breathing, pausing before responding, and maintaining a steady tone of voice can help manage emotional responses. A composed leader can act as an anchor in stormy situations, providing stability and clarity.

For instance, I recall a challenging situation where two parents requested a meeting to discuss the bullying of two of their primary-aged children. Ironically, it was their children who were known for bullying others. There had been several meetings and email exchanges with the mother about this issue.

My head of primary handled the situation, but the mother remained dissatisfied. Adding to the complexity, the father was the leader of a notorious local bikie gang and had a history of violence, including allegations of shooting a fellow bikie club member. During the meeting, both parents were aggressive, and the conversation was laden with expletives.

Despite the intense atmosphere, I maintained my calm, staying seated in a position that would allow me to defend myself if necessary. By remaining composed, I was able to let the parents express their grievances fully, and the meeting concluded without any physical confrontation. This experience underscored the importance of composure in leadership, especially in volatile situations.

Conveying messages effectively – clarity and empathy

Effective communication is about what is said and how it is said. In conflict situations, clarity and empathy are essential. Leaders must ensure that their messages are clear, concise, and free from jargon or ambiguity. This clarity helps prevent further misunderstandings. Equally important is the tone of the communication. Empathetic communication acknowledges others' perspectives and emotions, validating their experiences. This does not mean agreeing with them, but it shows respect for their point of view. Effective communicators also use "I" statements (e.g., "I feel", "I believe") rather than "you" statements (e.g., "You always", "You never"), which can come across as accusatory.

In conclusion, navigating the storm of conflict requires more than just managerial skills; it demands high emotional intelligence and communication finesse. By mastering the art of active listening, maintaining composure, and conveying messages with clarity and empathy, educational leaders can effectively manage conflicts, turning challenging situations into opportunities for growth and understanding.

Case study – navigating communication challenges during the pandemic

The Covid-19 pandemic brought unprecedented challenges to the education sector worldwide. As a school principal during this tumultuous period, I was faced with the difficult task of implementing and communicating new policies to ensure the safety and well-being of our school community. One such policy was to limit physical attendance at school to children of parents who were frontline workers, a decision that was necessary to reduce the spread of the virus but one that I knew would be challenging to convey to all parents.

The primary challenge was communicating this significant change effectively to the parents. I anticipated various reactions, from understanding and support to frustration and disagreement. The task was not only to convey the decision but also to manage the emotional responses and concerns of the parents, ensuring they felt supported and heard during this difficult time.

Approach and implementation
1. **Preparation and strategy development.** Knowing the sensitivity of the situation, I spent time preparing a clear and empathetic communication strategy. This involved consulting with educational authorities, health experts, and our school's leadership team to ensure the message was accurate and aligned with broader public health directives.
2. **Clear and empathetic communication.** I addressed the parents through various channels – an email, a letter home, and an online meeting. In each, I clearly explained the rationale behind the decision, emphasising the importance of safeguarding the health of our students, staff, and the wider community. I acknowledged the challenges this would pose to many families and expressed my empathy and understanding of their potential concerns.
3. **Active listening and feedback.** Following the announcement, I organised virtual feedback sessions and made myself available for one-on-one conversations. This allowed parents to voice their concerns and for me to listen actively, demonstrating that their opinions were valued and considered.
4. **Ongoing support and adaptability.** Recognising the ongoing nature of the pandemic, I ensured that the communication lines remained open for further feedback and questions. We also adapted our approach as the situation evolved, keeping the parents informed and involved in the decision-making process.

The decision, while difficult, was successfully implemented, with a majority of parents expressing their understanding and cooperation. The open and empathetic communication approach fostered a sense of community and mutual support, reinforcing the school's commitment to the well-being of all its members.

Lessons learned
1. Clear, empathetic communication is vital in managing sensitive decisions.
2. Active listening and providing platforms for feedback are essential in maintaining trust and respect in a school community.
3. Flexibility and adaptability are key in leadership, especially during times of crisis.

6.3 Negotiating with finesse

Negotiation is an art, especially in school leadership where diverse stakeholder interests often intersect and sometimes conflict. This subchapter goes into effective negotiation techniques that are crucial for managing challenging stakeholder interactions. The focus is on developing win-win strategies, understanding stakeholder needs, and mastering conflict de-escalation.

Win-win strategies

The goal of negotiation in schools should not be to "win" at the expense of others but to find solutions that benefit all parties involved. This requires creativity and an open-minded approach to problem-solving. Win-win strategies involve looking beyond the immediate conflict to understand stakeholders' underlying needs and concerns, and then crafting solutions that address these needs.

Understanding stakeholder needs

Effective negotiation hinges on deeply understanding what stakeholders truly value and need. This involves active listening, empathy, and the ability to read between the lines. Leaders must strive to understand the motivations and priorities of stakeholders, which can often differ from their stated positions.

Conflict de-escalation

In negotiations, emotions can run high. A key skill is the ability to de-escalate conflict, maintaining a calm and respectful atmosphere. This involves managing one's own emotions, as well as recognising and responding appropriately to the emotions of others. De-escalation techniques such as pausing, reframing, and using neutral language can help to diffuse tension and keep the discussion constructive.

Negotiating with finesse requires a combination of strategic thinking, emotional intelligence, and a genuine commitment to finding mutually beneficial solutions. By mastering these techniques, educational leaders can navigate the complexities of stakeholder interactions with greater confidence and effectiveness.

Let's unpack active listening

From experience, active listening is one effective and proven strategy for de-escalating a tense situation. This involves more than just hearing the words the other person is saying; it is about fully engaging with and understanding their perspective. Here is how active listening can be a powerful tool in conflict de-escalation.

1. **Give full attention.** Make eye contact, nod, and show that you fully focus on the speaker. This conveys respect and willingness to understand their point of view.
2. **Reflect back.** Paraphrase what you have heard in your own words. This shows that you are trying to understand their message and helps clarify any misunderstandings.
3. **Validate their feelings.** Acknowledge the emotions they are expressing, whether they are feeling frustration, anger, or disappointment. Validation doesn't mean you agree with their view, but it shows that you recognise their feelings as valid.
4. **Ask open-ended questions.** Encourage them to share more about their feelings and perspectives. This can provide deeper insight into the root of the conflict and show your interest in their viewpoint.
5. **Avoid interrupting.** Let them speak without interruption. Interrupting can escalate the situation, as it may be perceived as dismissiveness.
6. **Respond empathetically.** Respond with empathy after they have finished speaking. Show that you understand their feelings and that their concerns are important to you.

By actively listening, you can help the other person feel heard and understood, which can significantly reduce tension and pave the way for a more productive and constructive dialogue.

6.4 Cultivating consensus and cooperation

Cultivating consensus and cooperation among diverse stakeholders is an important objective. This subchapter focuses on strategies to build unity and foster collaborative environments. Key to this process is inclusive dialogue, acknowledging diverse viewpoints, and collaborative decision-making.

The foundation of consensus-building is creating an environment where every stakeholder feels they have a voice. Inclusive dialogue involves actively inviting and valuing contributions from all groups, especially those who might typically be underrepresented. This approach ensures that a broad range of perspectives is considered, enriching the decision-making process and building a sense of shared ownership over outcomes.

Finally, fostering collaboration in decision-making is key. This involves moving beyond mere consultation to actively co-creating solutions with stakeholders. Techniques such as brainstorming sessions, working groups, and consensus-building workshops can be effective. When stakeholders are involved in the decision-making process, they are more likely to support and champion the outcomes.

Cultivating consensus and cooperation is not a one-time effort but a continuous process that requires commitment and skill. By embracing inclusive dialogue, acknowledging diverse viewpoints, and engaging in collaborative decision-making, educational leaders can create a more unified and effective educational community.

Acknowledging diverse viewpoints

Recognising and respecting diverse viewpoints is crucial in building consensus. It is about understanding that each stakeholder brings unique experiences and insights. Acknowledging these differences, rather than seeking to minimise them, can lead to more creative and effective solutions. This approach requires patience, empathy, and a willingness to find common ground, even when opinions diverge.

Example from my work

Here is a short script that demonstrates how to acknowledge diverse viewpoints in a conversation.

> **Me (as principal):** *I really think we should focus our project on increasing digital marketing efforts. It's the most effective way to reach our target audience these days.*
>
> **Marketing Manager (MM):** *That's a valid point about digital marketing, and I see its potential. However, from my experience working with our older customer segments, traditional media like print and radio still hold significant value. How can we incorporate that into our strategy?*
>
> **Me:** *I hadn't considered the impact on our older customer segments. You're right; they might respond better to traditional media. Perhaps we could balance our approach, using both digital and traditional methods tailored to different segments?*
>
> **MM:** *I like that idea. It's a good way to leverage the strengths of both methods and reach a wider audience. We could use analytics to measure the effectiveness in each segment and adjust our strategy as needed.*

In this situation, my marketing manager and I acknowledged and respected each other's viewpoints, leading to a collaborative solution that integrated diverse perspectives.

6.5 Managing stakeholder dynamics – balancing boundaries and navigating opposition

In educational leadership, balancing expectations with boundaries and navigating resistance and opposition are intertwined challenges that require strategic communication, empathy, and firm leadership. This subchapter analyses the complexities of managing stakeholder dynamics in schools.

Understanding and enforcing boundaries

- **Clear communication** – establishing and communicating clear limitations and boundaries.
- **Enforcing boundaries** – upholding school values and safety through firm leadership, as exemplified by handling a disruptive parent by imposing necessary restrictions.
- **Managing disappointments** – recognising the potential repercussions of enforcing boundaries and preparing for ongoing challenges.

Strategies for effective stakeholder management

- **Educating and informing** – providing clear, factual information to dispel misconceptions and build understanding.
- **Change management techniques** – utilising strategies to ease transitions and reduce resistance.
- **Root cause analysis** – conducting analyses to understand deeper issues behind resistance.

Building consensus and managing long-term challenges

- **Acknowledging and addressing concerns** – recognising valid concerns and addressing them directly.
- **Seeking common ground** – finding areas of agreement or shared goals as a basis for consensus.
- **Steadfast leadership and trust building** – maintaining firm, consistent leadership while building trust through honesty and transparency.

Scenario – resistance stemming from personal values in a school setting

A school in my area had introduced a new policy to incorporate gender-neutral uniforms years ago. The policy aimed to promote inclusivity and respect for gender diversity. However, Mr Thompson, a long-serving and respected teacher known for his traditional views, expressed strong resistance to the change.

During a staff meeting, Mr Thompson voiced his opposition, stating that the new uniform policy contradicted his personal belief in traditional gender norms. He argued that the school should maintain these norms rather than adopt what he perceived as a radical approach.

The school's leadership team recognised that Mr Thompson's resistance stemmed from his personal values. They understood that his long-held beliefs about gender roles influenced his opposition to the policy change.

The principal decided to have a one-on-one conversation with Mr Thompson. The aim was not to directly challenge his personal beliefs but to discuss how the school's commitment to inclusivity and respect for all students could coexist with diverse personal values. The principal also planned to offer professional development sessions for the staff, focusing on understanding and respecting gender diversity, to create a supportive environment for such policy changes.

Through this approach, the school leadership hoped to address Mr Thompson's concerns while reinforcing the importance of the school's inclusive values. The goal was to find a balance where Mr Thompson felt his values were acknowledged without compromising the school's commitment to inclusivity and respect for all students' identities. As a principal, it was crucial to make bold decisions that benefited the school community. It was also important to engage constructively with opposing views and turn potential conflicts into opportunities for growth and positive change. This approach highlighted the significance of preserving the integrity of the school's ethos while adapting to the evolving needs and concerns of its community.

Interpersonal and external relationship management

In addition to the diplomatic skills mentioned earlier, effective school leadership also requires a robust understanding of political savvy. This term, often perceived pejoratively, is in fact a critical skill set for navigating the complex web of relationships and power dynamics inherent in schools, especially in schools that are deeply integrated within their communities, such as faith-based schools.

Political savvy does not mean compromising one's values, but rather involves strategically manoeuvring through institutional and community politics to secure favourable outcomes for the school. This involves understanding the motivations of different stakeholders and tactfully aligning them with the school's goals.

For example, a principal might need to foster strong relationships with local leaders, parent groups, and faith organisations, ensuring that the school's initiatives are supported and effectively implemented. This skill allows leaders to not only survive but thrive in positions where external pressures and expectations are high, ensuring the school's vision is realised without losing sight of its core values.

The importance of skilled listening and discernment in resolving conflicts effectively

In managing conflicts, particularly with tricky stakeholders, it is imperative for a principal to possess the ability to distinguish between the "presenting issue" – the explicit complaint or problem initially brought forward – and the "underlying issue" – the deeper, often unspoken reasons behind the conflict.

This distinction is crucial, as addressing only the surface issues without uncovering the root causes can lead to temporary resolutions that fail to prevent future disputes. The skill of discerning these underlying issues requires highly developed listening abilities, often referred to as "active" or "empathetic" listening. This involves not only hearing the words that are said but also interpreting the emotions and motivations that underpin them. By engaging in this level of listening, a principal can better understand the true nature of the conflict, facilitating a more effective and enduring resolution. This process often uncovers emotional needs, historical grievances, or miscommunications that, if addressed properly, can transform a contentious relationship into a constructive one. Therefore, training in and practising these listening skills should be a priority for school leaders aiming to adeptly navigate the complexities of stakeholder management.

6.6 Turning challenges into lessons

In educational leadership, difficult stakeholder interactions are not just challenges to be overcome; they are opportunities for significant learning and growth. This subchapter explores how leaders can transform these challenging encounters into valuable lessons, enhancing their personal and professional development. We will delve into reflective practices and discuss how these experiences can be leveraged for growth using a structured approach, as shown in the table below.

Difficult stakeholder interactions	Reflective practice	Professional growth
1. Resistance to policy changes	• Examining the reasons behind the resistance • Assessing the effectiveness of communication strategies • Considering alternative approaches	• Improved skills in change management and communication • Enhanced ability to anticipate and address stakeholder concerns • Greater resilience in facing opposition
2. Conflict with a parent or guardian	• Reflecting on the interaction dynamics • Evaluating personal emotional responses • Seeking feedback from trusted colleagues	• Enhanced conflict resolution and negotiation skills • Increased emotional intelligence and self-awareness • Improved ability to maintain professionalism under stress
3. Disagreement with school board decisions	• Analysing the decision-making process • Identifying personal biases and assumptions • Considering the broader perspective and long-term implications	• Strengthened strategic thinking and decision-making skills • Deeper understanding of governance and board dynamics • Enhanced ability to balance diverse perspectives and interests

Reflective practice is a powerful tool for professional development. It involves taking a step back to critically analyse our actions, decisions, and outcomes. This process helps us understand what happened and why it happened, enabling us to learn from these experiences. Reflective practice can take many forms, such as journaling, discussions with mentors, or formal debriefing sessions.

Leveraging experiences for personal and professional growth

Every difficult interaction with stakeholders provides us with a wealth of information and insights. We can extract valuable lessons by approaching these situations with a mindset geared towards learning. This might involve identifying areas for skill enhancement, recognising our personal strengths and weaknesses, or gaining a deeper understanding of the complexities of educational leadership.

Transforming challenges into opportunities

Turning challenges into lessons requires a conscious effort. It involves:

- **Adopting a growth mindset** – viewing challenges as opportunities for learning rather than as setbacks.
- **Seeking feedback and support** – engaging with mentors, peers, or professional coaches for different perspectives and advice.
- **Applying lessons learned** – actively applying the insights gained from reflective practices in future interactions and decision-making processes.

In conclusion, difficult stakeholder interactions, though often daunting, are invaluable in our journey as a leader. By engaging in reflective practices and viewing these challenges as learning opportunities, we can continually evolve, enhancing our effectiveness and impact in our role.

6.7 Stakeholder engagement

Case study – navigating parental concerns in curriculum changes

At one of my schools, the introduction of a new, progressive mathematics curriculum was met with significant resistance from a group of parents. These parents were concerned that the new curriculum deviated too much from traditional methods and could negatively impact their children's learning outcomes and university preparation. "It doesn't resemble how maths was taught when I was at school," claimed one oppositional parent.

I recognised the importance of addressing these concerns promptly and effectively. I understood that parents are key stakeholders in the educational process and that their support is crucial for the successful implementation of new initiatives. I employed several strategies to manage this tricky stakeholder situation:

- **Open communication forums** – a series of meetings where parents could voice their concerns. These forums were designed to be open

and non-confrontational, allowing for a constructive dialogue between parents and the school leadership.
- **Evidence-based responses** – data and research supporting the efficacy of the new curriculum were presented to parents. I used research and reports from experts in mathematics education to explain the long-term benefits of progressive learning methods in mathematics.
- **Pilot program results** – prior to the full implementation, the curriculum was piloted in a few classes. The head of maths was able to share positive feedback and improvements in student engagement and understanding from these pilot classes.
- **Parent involvement in monitoring** – a (small) committee of interested parents was formed to monitor the rollout of the new curriculum. This committee was involved in regular check-ins and feedback sessions, making them active participants in the implementation process.
- **Continued traditional support** – to address concerns about whether students were prepared for university maths, I offered supplementary traditional maths classes and resources for students who wished to pursue them.

This multi-faceted approach helped in easing the concerns of the parents. The communication forums and involvement in the monitoring committee made the parents feel heard and valued, while the evidence-based responses and pilot program results helped in building trust in the new curriculum. The option to access traditional resources ensured that the parents felt their children's needs were being catered to.

Practical insights and takeaways
1. **Stakeholder engagement is crucial.** Effective stakeholder engagement, especially in situations of change, is essential. Understanding stakeholders' concerns and addressing them respectfully can lead to more harmonious and effective outcomes.
2. **Transparency builds trust.** Open and honest communication fosters a sense of trust and partnership between the school and its stakeholders.
3. **Inclusivity in decision-making.** Involving stakeholders in the monitoring and feedback process can greatly enhance the acceptance and success of new initiatives.
4. **Flexibility and compromise.** Offering compromises, like supplementary traditional classes in this case, can be an effective way to balance innovation with stakeholder comfort levels.

5. **Evidence-based approach.** Utilising data and expert opinions can be persuasive in validating new approaches and alleviating concerns based on misinformation or fear of change.

This case study demonstrates that, with thoughtful strategies and a commitment to open dialogue, even the most challenging stakeholder situations in a school setting can be managed effectively.

6.8 Takeaway – framework for preparing for future stakeholder challenges

Here is a framework that helped me and my executive leaders anticipate potential conflicts and employ proactive stakeholder engagement strategies:

1. **Conduct regular stakeholder analysis**

   Insight: Identify all potential stakeholders (parents, students, staff, community members, etc.).

   Application: Understand their interests, concerns, and the level of influence they have on the school environment.

2. **Develop a proactive communication plan**

   Insight: Establish regular communication channels (newsletters, emails, social media, meetings).

   Application: Share updates, successes, challenges, and future plans to keep stakeholders informed and involved.

3. **Create a feedback loop**

   Insight: Implement mechanisms for stakeholders to voice their opinions and concerns (surveys, suggestion boxes, forums).

   Application: Regularly review and address feedback in a timely and respectful manner.

4. **Engage in active listening**

   Insight: Practise active listening during interactions with stakeholders.

   Application: Show empathy and understanding of their perspectives and concerns.

5. **Foster a collaborative environment**

   Insight: Encourage stakeholder participation in decision-making processes.

   Application: Organise workshops or focus groups on key issues or changes.

6. **Provide educational opportunities**

    Insight: Offer informational sessions or workshops for stakeholders to understand educational trends, policies, and the rationale behind decisions.

    Application: Use experts or credible sources to support these educational initiatives.

7. **Anticipate and plan for change**

    Insight: Stay informed about potential changes in the educational landscape (policy changes, technological advancements, societal shifts).

    Application: Develop contingency plans for how these changes might impact stakeholders and how to address their concerns.

8. **Build strong relationships**

    Insight: Develop and maintain positive relationships with all stakeholders.

    Application: Show appreciation for their contributions and acknowledge their role in the school's success.

9. **Monitor and evaluate engagement strategies**

    Insight: Regularly assess the effectiveness of stakeholder engagement strategies.

    Application: Make adjustments based on outcomes and feedback.

10. **Be transparent and honest**

    Insight: Maintain transparency in all dealings with stakeholders.

    Application: Be honest about challenges and limitations while remaining optimistic about solutions and opportunities.

11. **Develop a culture of respect and inclusivity**

    Insight: Promote a school culture that values diversity, inclusivity, and mutual respect.

    Application: Ensure that all stakeholder voices are valued and considered.

By following this framework, principals can proactively prepare for and effectively manage future stakeholder challenges, fostering a more harmonious and productive school environment.

CHAPTER 7

THE BALANCING ACT
Managing resources and priorities

This chapter explores the vital work of principals in a core area of leadership: resource management. School principals often find themselves in the situation where stakeholder demands for resources outweigh the income to pay for them. The ability to prioritise and judiciously allocate resources becomes not just a skill but an art. This chapter guides you through the strategies and insights necessary to master this balancing act, ensuring that your school not only survives fiscal constraints and educational expectations but thrives.

7.1 Understanding school budget basics

Navigating the complexities of school budgeting is a fundamental skill for effective school leadership. A well-managed budget ensures the school's smooth running and lays the groundwork for academic excellence and student success.

At its core, a school budget is a financial plan that reflects the educational goals and priorities of the school. It is a blueprint that details how funds will be obtained and allocated to support various school activities and programs. Understanding this plan is vital for aligning financial resources with the school's strategic objectives.

The primary sources of school funding can vary depending on the type of school (public, independent, or systemic) and location. For most public schools, funding primarily comes from state and federal government allocations, which are often determined by student enrolment numbers, demographic factors, and specific educational needs.

Independent schools, on the other hand, rely more heavily on tuition fees, donations, grants, and fundraising efforts. Each source comes with its own set of regulations and limitations, which are crucial to understand for effective budget management.

The income for an independent school usually comes from four main sources:

1. Parents paying tuition fees.
2. Commonwealth recurrent income.
3. State recurrent income.
4. Private sources, such as philanthropic contributions.

The proportion of government funding to total income varies significantly among independent schools, depending on factors such as location, socio-economic status of the school community, and specific needs of the students.

Here is the financial data (from 2022) for an independent school in a provincial NSW city with an enrolment of 1100 students and an ICSEA (Index of Community Socio-Educational Advantage) value of 1112. The national average is 1000.

Net recurrent income	Total	Per student
Australian government recurrrent funding	$10,003,995	$8,988
State/territory government recurring funding	$2,517,535	$2,262
Fees, charges and parent contributions	$15,973,150	$14,351
Other private sources	$502,891	$452
Total gross income	**$28,997,571**	**$26,054**

In this school, 43 percent of the total net recurrent income comes from government funding, with 55 percent of income coming from parents paying fees.

For independent schools, government funding typically ranges from about 20 to 50 percent of their total income. Schools in higher socio-economic areas tend to receive less government funding as a percentage of total income, relying more heavily on fees paid by parents. Conversely, schools in lower socio-economic areas or those serving specific groups with additional needs may receive a higher proportion of government funding.

This range is quite broad due to the diversity of independent schools in Australia, including their size, mission, and the demographics they serve (ISA, 2024).

The expenditure side of a school budget can be categorised into several key areas:

1. **Staffing costs.** This typically represents the largest portion of the budget, covering salaries and benefits for teachers, administrative staff, and support personnel.
2. **Operational expenses.** These are the costs associated with the day-to-day running of the school, including utilities, maintenance, and administrative and tuition expenses.
3. **Curricular and extracurricular programs.** Funds allocated here support academic programs, sports, arts, and other student activities.
4. **Technology and equipment.** Technology, equipment, and infrastructure investment is essential for maintaining a modern educational environment.
5. **Professional development.** A portion of the budget is dedicated to the ongoing training and development of staff.
6. **Capital expenditures.** These are funds set aside for long-term investments like building renovations or major equipment purchases.

In the example above, 70 percent of expenditure is on staff salaries, leave benefits, and superannuation.

It is important for school leaders not only to understand these categories but also to recognise the dynamic and interconnected nature of school budgeting. Changes in one area can have ripple effects throughout the budget. Therefore, a holistic and flexible approach is essential for effective budget management.

By grasping these foundational concepts, school leaders can begin to navigate the complexities of school budgeting, aligning financial resources with their school's mission and ensuring a stable and prosperous educational environment.

Budget for a K-12 school

I have created a budget report on the next page which I have modelled on a school with 500 students and a full-time-equivalent staff of 70. The budget breakdown is modelled for a school with an ICSEA value of 1140 (the national average is 1000). Here is the guide to understanding ICSEA values: https://myschool.edu.au/media/1900/guide-to-understanding-icsea-values-2023.pdf. A school with an ICSEA of 1140 would be regarded as a school with a community that has a high capacity to pay school fees.

Here are some questions you would ask yourself about the budget if you were the principal or on the board's finance committee:

1. **Analysis of income sources.** Can you identify and analyse the various sources of income listed in the budget? How do these income streams contribute to the overall financial stability of the school, and what potential risks or dependencies can you identify?
2. **Expenditure priorities.** Examine the expenditure categories in the budget. What do these expenses reveal about the school's priorities and strategic objectives? Are there any areas where the allocation of funds seems disproportionately high or low?
3. **Cost-benefit considerations.** Choose a specific expenditure item and discuss the potential cost-benefit implications. How might this expense contribute to the school's long-term goals, and what are the possible returns on this investment?
4. **Financial health assessment.** Based on the budget, how would you assess the financial health of the school? Consider factors like the balance between income and expenses, the presence of surplus or deficit, and the allocation of funds towards savings or debt reduction.
5. **Recommendations for improvement.** If you were to suggest one or two improvements or changes to this budget, what would they be and why? How would your recommendations enhance the financial management or strategic goals of the school?

	2022 Budget
INCOME	
Tuition fees	7,159,034
Rebates	(353,560)
Regional recurrent funding	1,113,743
Commonwealth recurrent funding	4,330,559
Capital donations	12,000
Interest received	3,000
Income – other	22,970
Total operating income	**12,287,746**
SALARIES AND WAGES	
Teachers (inc ELC)	5,676,677
Relief teachers (inc ELC)	110,682
Technicians and assistants	741,681
Administration and executive	821,062
Buildings and maintenance	384,400
Relief and extra hours non-teachers	14,834
Superannuation	790,484
Annual leave loading	100,813
Long service leave	85,612
Total salary and wages	**8,726,244**
EXPENSES	
Tuition expenses	638,570
Student activities	332,808
Other operational	413,676
Administrative expenses	993,982
Total operating expenses	**2,379,036**
BUILDINGS AND GROUNDS	**691,416**
Borrowing costs	164,909
Provision for doubtful debts and bad debt expense	(15,000)
Depreciation	933,855
Total other	**1,083,764**
Operating surplus/(deficit)	**(592,713)**

7.2 Strategic budget planning

Aligning budget with strategic goals

A school's budget is more than a mere financial document; it is a statement of priorities and a roadmap for future growth and development. When a school's budget is closely aligned with its strategic goals, it ensures that resources are being allocated effectively to areas that will significantly impact student success and institutional advancement.

For instance, if a school's strategic goal is to enhance STEM education, the budget should reflect increased allocations towards science labs, technology upgrades, and STEM teacher training. This alignment not only streamlines resource allocation but also helps communicate the school's commitment to these goals to all stakeholders, including staff, parents, and the wider community.

Methods for effective long-term financial planning

1. **Comprehensive needs assessment.** Begin with thoroughly assessing the school's current resources, needs, and future aspirations. This assessment should encompass academic programs, infrastructure, technology, staff development, and student services. Understanding the gap between current resources and future needs is crucial in setting realistic and strategic budget priorities.
2. **Stakeholder involvement.** Engage various stakeholders in the budget planning process. This can include teachers, administrative staff, parents, and even students. Their insights can provide valuable perspectives on where the school should invest its resources.
3. **Scenario planning.** Develop multiple budget scenarios based on different funding levels or priorities. This approach allows school leaders to foresee the potential impacts of various budget choices and make informed decisions. It also prepares the school to adapt to unforeseen financial challenges or opportunities.
4. **Prioritisation of expenditures.** With limited resources, prioritising expenditures becomes essential. Expenditures should be categorised into "must-haves", "nice-to-haves", and "future considerations". This categorisation helps in making tough decisions when resources are constrained.
5. **Multi-year budgeting.** Instead of focusing solely on the immediate fiscal year, adopt a multi-year budgeting approach. This method allows

for better planning and preparation for large-scale investments and can smooth out fluctuations in funding sources over time.
6. **Regular review and adjustments.** The budget should be a living document, subject to regular review and adjustments as needed. Changes in student enrolment, funding sources, and other external factors may necessitate revisions to the budget.
7. **Transparency and communication.** Maintain transparency in budgeting and communicate the rationale behind budget decisions to all stakeholders. This openness builds trust and ensures community support for the school's financial plans.

Strategic budget planning is integral to the success of a school. By aligning the budget with strategic goals and employing effective long-term financial planning methods, school leaders can ensure that they are not only managing the present needs efficiently but are also paving the way for future growth and success. This approach to budgeting helps transform financial constraints into opportunities for strategic innovation and development.

7.3 Navigating budget constraints and challenges – a personal case study

Adapting to funding method changes in an independent school

During my time as principal at a prominent, regional independent school, we encountered a substantial financial hurdle following a shift in the Commonwealth Government's funding approach.

From 2020, the Australian Government began phasing in the new Direct Measure of Income (DMI) methodology (https://isa.edu.au/our-sector/funding/school-funding-model/). The new DMI methodology uses the personal income tax data of parents and guardians to calculate the median income in a school, which is used to determine the funding level for the school.

The DMI methodology requires the collection of the names and addresses of students' parents and guardians from non-government schools every year. These are provided to the Commonwealth Department of Education as part of the student address collection. These names and addresses are then linked to personal income tax records as part of the Multi-Agency Data Integration Project (MADIP), a secure ABS data environment which enables linkages between large government data sets.

Along with dozens of principals in regional independent schools, I was a strident opponent of the changes. Despite our best efforts to make a case to government, our efforts went unheard. I could only prepare my school for the change. We would lose millions of dollars in funding, and our revenue base would be severely hit.

As we faced the new funding methodology, it became imperative to strategically reassess our financial management practices. Despite the challenges posed by reduced funding, our commitment remained to uphold high educational standards and maintain the breadth of programs offered.

Strategies considered

I was considering a range of strategies, developing a plan to mitigate the loss of income. As it turned out, I finished my time at this school before the introduction of the changes and before I had to roll out my plans, but here are some of those strategies that I was considering:

- **Strategic financial reassessment.** I led a thorough review of our budget, focusing on expenditures that were crucial for student learning and essential school operations. I identified non-essential expenses that could be reduced where possible.
- **Engaging the school community.** I knew I would have to leverage the strength of our school community by transparently sharing the financial challenges and the rationale behind them. I would have encouraged feedback and participation from parents, alumni, and local businesses to help the school navigate through this period of transition.
- **Seeking alternative revenue streams.** I planned on working with the business manager (BM) at the time to explore new sources of revenue. This would have included applying for grants, initiating targeted fundraising efforts, and soliciting donations and support from our alumni network. The school board were completely aware of the changes and the financial impact on the school's operations, and I would have commenced work with the finance committee to address the challenges.
- **Optimising operational efficiencies.** I planned on working closely with the BM to implement cost-saving strategies across all areas of school operations. I had my eye on adopting more energy-efficient practices, renegotiating contracts to secure better rates from vendors, and increasing our use of digital resources to cut costs.

- **Collaborative cost-saving innovations.** Our teaching staff would have been instrumental in this process. We would have looked at how the curriculum was developed and delivered and at our staff:student ratios to find savings without compromising education outcomes.
- **Transparent and inclusive decision-making.** My objective was to maintain an inclusive approach to decision-making during this challenging time. Regular meetings with various stakeholders would have ensured that everyone was well-informed and their insights were considered in our decision-making processes.

This case study from my time at an independent school emphasises the significance of adaptive leadership and strategic financial management in responding to external changes in funding. My weapons for overcoming financial challenges and fostering resilience would have been: effective communication, community engagement, and innovative resource management.

7.4 Resource allocation and optimisation – a real-life example

Balancing resource allocation in music, sport, and academic programs

One of the schools I led faced scrutiny over our budget allocations, particularly the perceived imbalance between funding for music and sports programs versus teaching and learning resources. This scenario provides a real-life context to explore the principles of equitable and efficient resource allocations and how to assess and prioritise these allocations effectively.

The critique centred on the belief that substantial resources were being funnelled into music and sports at the expense of academic resources. This perception highlighted the need for a more balanced and transparent approach to resource allocation that aligned with the school's comprehensive educational goals.

Principles of equitable and efficient resource allocation

1. **Comprehensive needs assessment.** I began with a thorough assessment of the needs across all departments, including academics, music, and sports. This assessment was crucial to understand the resources required to achieve optimal outcomes in each area.

2. **Stakeholder engagement.** It was essential to involve teachers, parents, and students in discussions about resource allocation. This engagement helped to clarify misconceptions and provided diverse perspectives on the value of different programs.
3. **Aligning allocation with strategic goals.** I ensured that resource allocation decisions were aligned with the school's strategic educational goals. While music and sports were vital for holistic development, academic excellence remained a core objective. I had to find a balance.
4. **Balancing short-term needs with long-term goals.** I carefully balanced immediate resource requirements with our long-term vision for the school. This approach allowed us to allocate resources not just based on current demands but also in anticipation of future needs.

Strategies for resource optimisation

1. **Transparent communication.** The BM and I improved transparency around budget decisions. Communicating the rationale behind allocations helped mitigate misconceptions and built trust within the school community.
2. **Cross-departmental collaboration.** Encouraging collaboration between departments allowed for more creative use of resources. For instance, integrating music and sports themes into academic projects created a more interconnected educational experience without additional costs.
3. **Regular review and adjustment.** The budget was reviewed regularly to ensure it remained responsive to changing needs and priorities. This dynamic approach allowed us to reallocate resources efficiently as needs evolved. This was particularly important in January each year, once we were certain about our enrolment and staffing. A budget is usually accepted in August–October of the year prior, so it makes sense to revisit the budget at the start of the year. Some schools also do a May forecast once the first rounds of state and commonwealth funding have been confirmed and banked.

Through these strategies, our school achieved a more balanced and equitable distribution of resources. The perception of favouring certain programs over others was addressed by demonstrating a commitment to all aspects of student development and learning.

This real-life example from my school illustrates the importance of equitable and efficient resource allocation. By engaging stakeholders, aligning resources with strategic goals, and maintaining transparency, schools can effectively manage resources to support diverse programs while upholding academic excellence.

7.5 Engaging stakeholders in budgeting and resource decisions

The process of developing and managing a school budget is not just a task for the finance department; it is a collaborative endeavour that requires the active participation of various stakeholders. As leaders, it is crucial to involve all budget holders in the process. My process was to start from a zero base, to ensure that each dollar spent aligned with the school's strategic goals and educational mission.

"Budget holders" are typically department heads or managers responsible for managing the finances of specific areas within the school, such as academics, sports, arts, or facilities. They are tasked with planning and overseeing their respective budgets, ensuring that expenditures align with the school's strategic objectives.

The role of leaders in the budgeting process

Leadership in budgeting extends beyond mere oversight; it involves guiding the conversation, setting priorities, and ensuring transparency and accountability. One effective approach is to start budgeting from a zero base. This means that instead of basing the new budget on last year's figures, each department starts from zero and justifies every expense. This approach necessitates thoroughly reviewing all activities and resources, encouraging efficiency, and aligning expenditures with the school's current priorities.

Involving all budget holders

Involving all budget holders in the budgeting process is essential. This practice ensures that every department's needs and challenges are considered and that the final budget is comprehensive and balanced. Regular meetings with key budget holders are not just administrative necessities but opportunities for collaboration and insight. Bringing together different departments in one room gives a broader perspective of the school's overall needs and priorities.

During these meetings, leaders can share the holistic budget and discuss budget constraints. It is essential to be transparent about the overall financial health of the school and any external factors impacting the budget, such as changes in funding or economic conditions. This transparency helps build trust and understanding among the stakeholders.

"Stakeholders" in this context extend beyond the finance team to include anyone with a vested interest in the school's success and operational efficiency. This group may encompass teachers, staff, students, parents, and the school board. All play a critical role in the school's ecosystem, influencing and being affected by how resources are allocated and priorities are managed.

Budget 101 education

These budget meetings also provide an excellent opportunity for "Budget 101" education. Many budget holders, especially those from non-financial backgrounds, may not fully understand the complexities of school finance. Leaders can use this time to educate them about basic financial concepts, budgeting processes, and financial accountability. This educational aspect empowers department heads to make more informed decisions and propose realistic budgets for their areas.

Methods for effective communication

Effective communication is paramount in involving stakeholders in budget decisions. This can be achieved through a variety of methods:

- **Regular updates.** Keep stakeholders informed about the budgeting process through regular updates via emails or dedicated meetings.
- **Feedback mechanisms.** Establish channels for stakeholders to voice their concerns and suggestions regarding the budget. I used surveys and email feedback, as well as the occasional open forum.
- **Interactive workshops.** Conduct workshops where stakeholders can learn about the budgeting process, ask questions, and provide input. Parents are far more likely to accept fee increases year-by-year if they have a good grasp of the school's budget and how their fees are used and invested. I would host a welcome reception for parents at the start of each school year and at that session provide parents with insightful data about our school's budget; I know they appreciated it.

- **Clear documentation.** Provide clear, easy-to-understand documentation of the budget, highlighting key areas of expenditure and revenue.
- **One-on-one discussions.** For more sensitive topics or where specific departments are significantly impacted, one-on-one discussions may be more appropriate.

Engaging stakeholders in the budgeting and resource decision-making process is not just a good practice; it is essential for creating a budget that truly reflects the needs and goals of the school. By involving all budget holders, educating them, and maintaining open lines of communication, leaders can ensure a more effective, transparent, and collaborative budgeting process.

7.6 Monitoring, reporting, and accountability

The imperative of financial transparency and accountability in schools cannot be overstated. As stewards of public and private funds, principals are entrusted with ensuring that every dollar is spent wisely and ethically. This subchapter explores the importance of these principles, offering guidance on monitoring expenditures and reporting to stakeholders, and examines a real-life example that highlights the necessity for stringent financial oversight.

The importance of financial transparency and accountability

Transparency and accountability in financial matters are critical for maintaining the trust of stakeholders, including parents, staff, and the wider community. This trust is fundamental to the smooth operation and reputation of any school. It involves clear, open communication about how funds are being used and ensuring that expenditures align with the school's mission and objectives.

A cautionary tale – misuse of funds by a school bursar

A stark illustration of the consequences when transparency and accountability falter can be seen in the case of a school bursar at a regional boarding school. In this instance, the bursar, who also owned a farm, exploited his position by siphoning off school funds. He orchestrated this by purchasing products for his personal farm, disguising them as legitimate expenses for the school. Utilising the same suppliers as the school, he was able to make these transactions appear valid. By the time his actions were uncovered, he had illicitly diverted over $500,000 to his personal use.

Strategies for monitoring expenditures

1. **Regular financial audits.** Conduct regular, thorough audits of all school financial transactions. External audits can provide an unbiased review of financial practices.
2. **Segregation of duties.** Ensure that no single individual has control over all aspects of financial transactions to prevent mismanagement or fraud.
3. **Transparent procurement processes.** Implement clear procurement policies with checks and balances. Regularly review vendor relationships and pricing to ensure fairness and market competitiveness.
4. **Real-time financial monitoring systems.** Utilise financial software that allows for real-time monitoring of expenditures and alerts for unusual transactions.

Reporting to stakeholders

1. **Regular financial statements.** Provide periodic financial statements to the school board, parents, and other stakeholders, detailing income, expenditures, and comparisons to budgeted figures.
2. **Open forums.** Hold regular meetings or forums where stakeholders can review financial reports and ask questions.
3. **Accessible financial information.** Make financial information, such as budgets and expenditure reports, accessible to stakeholders through the school's website or upon request.
4. **Explaining variances.** When actual expenditures significantly deviate from the budget, provide clear explanations to stakeholders about the reasons for these variances.

The case of the school bursar at the regional boarding school serves as a potent reminder of the critical need for robust systems of financial monitoring, reporting, and accountability. By implementing rigorous financial controls and maintaining transparency with all stakeholders, schools can safeguard their resources, uphold their integrity, and ensure they continue serving their educational mission effectively.

7.7 Key takeaways

As I conclude this chapter here are the key takeaways to keep in mind:

- **Strategic alignment.** Ensure that budget planning aligns with your school's strategic goals. Every financial decision should support and advance these objectives.
- **Stakeholder involvement.** Engage all stakeholders, including staff, parents, and students, in the budgeting process for a more inclusive and balanced financial plan.
- **Transparency and communication.** Maintain transparency in financial matters. Regularly communicate with stakeholders about budgetary decisions and their implications.
- **Zero-based budgeting.** Consider adopting a zero-based budgeting approach where necessary, to align expenditures closely with current needs and priorities.
- **Financial accountability.** Establish strong systems for financial monitoring and accountability to prevent mismanagement and ensure ethical use of funds.
- **Regular audits and reviews.** Conduct regular financial audits and reviews to maintain financial health and address any discrepancies promptly.
- **Adaptability and resilience.** Be adaptable in financial planning and management. Be prepared to adjust and respond to unexpected financial challenges or changes in funding.
- **Invest in financial education.** Continuously educate yourself and your team on financial management to enhance decision-making skills and financial literacy.
- **Prioritise student outcomes.** In all financial decisions, prioritise initiatives and expenditures directly impacting student learning and outcomes.
- **Build trust through financial stewardship.** Demonstrate responsible financial stewardship to build trust within the school community and beyond.

Remember, effective resource management is a dynamic and ongoing process requiring continuous attention, assessment, and adjustment to meet the evolving needs of your school.

CHAPTER 8

CRISIS LEADERSHIP
Responding to challenges and emergencies

8.1 Steering through uncertainty

Navigating crises effectively is not just a skill but a necessity. Crisis leadership extends beyond conventional management; it demands prompt decision-making, adaptability, and an unwavering commitment to safeguarding the well-being of students and staff. Whether facing natural disasters, safety threats, or public health emergencies, the role of a principal becomes pivotal in steering the school through turmoil and uncertainty.

Crises can arise without warning, leaving little room for hesitation. In such moments, the actions and decisions of a school leader can have profound implications on the safety, stability, and recovery of the school community.

Structured around three real-life examples – a sudden and devastating flood, the aftermath of a violent storm, and the security threat posed by an escaped paedophile – this chapter provides an insightful exploration of crisis management in action. These scenarios illustrate not only the challenges and complexities inherent in crises but also the strategies and approaches that can lead to successful navigation and resolution. Through these examples, readers will gain valuable insights into the principles of effective crisis leadership, equipping them to handle emergencies with competence and composure.

8.2 Navigating natural disasters – the flood crisis

The day started like any other at our 32-acre school set on a sloping gradient from south to north, but what unfolded over the next hour was unprecedented. A record-breaking downpour, with over 1000 mm of rain, turned the school grounds and surrounding area into a watery chaos. The sheer volume of water overwhelmed drainage systems, causing rapid flooding that threatened the safety of students and staff. The school, unaccustomed to such extreme weather, faced an immediate and severe crisis.

As the rain intensified, it became clear that this was no ordinary storm. Our first priority was the safety of everyone on campus. We implemented our emergency lockdown procedure, an action we had rehearsed but never expected to use under such circumstances. I took command from the undercroft of the school library, a good vantage point.

The decision-making process in these initial moments was critical. We set up an emergency response team comprising senior staff members responsible for communicating with each classroom and ensuring that all students and teachers were accounted for. Teachers were instructed to move students to higher ground within the school buildings, away from windows and potential flooding areas.

Communication was key. Using the school's email network, we relayed instructions and reassured everyone that measures were being taken to ensure their safety. Our administrative staff contacted local emergency services and monitored weather updates, relaying information to the response team.

Once the rain subsided and it was deemed safe, we faced the next challenge: sending over 1000 students home. Many roads were impassable, and parents were understandably anxious. We coordinated with local bus services, which were rerouted to accommodate road closures, to transport students who lived further away. For students who walked or cycled to school, we set up a temporary shelter in the gymnasium and contacted their parents for pick-up.

The school premises suffered significant damage. The lower floors of several buildings were flooded, and debris littered the grounds. However, the immediate concern was assessing the structural integrity of the school buildings. We brought in engineers to ensure that the buildings were safe before allowing anyone to re-enter. We were able to achieve this inside two days, and with students at home we mitigated the risk.

While the flood was an unprecedented challenge for us, it was also a powerful learning experience. It reinforced the need for robust preparedness strategies and highlighted the strength and resilience of our school community in times of crisis.

8.3 Overcoming environmental catastrophes – the storm aftermath

This storm event is different to the flood event discussed in subchapter 8.2.

Our school was nestled in a serene suburban area; we had many large, tall gum trees. We experienced a violent storm that uprooted dozens of those ancient gum trees and wreaked havoc on the school's infrastructure. The storm, unpredictable and ferocious, hit the town late one afternoon, leaving a trail of destruction in its wake. The school, known for its expansive campus dotted with lush greenery, faced an unprecedented challenge: the aftermath of a storm that had transformed its landscape into a scene of chaos and danger. At the time, I was overseas studying IB schools abroad. Videos of the storms were being shown in European countries. I could only watch in despair. The leadership team back home were magnificent in my absence.

School closure and community response

The extent of the damage was evident at dawn. Massive gum trees, some over a century old, lay uprooted, blocking pathways, damaging buildings, and rendering the school grounds unsafe. The decision to close the school was immediate and unequivocal. Our priority was the safety of our students and staff, and with the school in such a state, resuming regular activities was out of the question.

However, the aftermath of the storm presented another significant challenge. The city was reeling from the storm's impact, and professional contractors were stretched thin, attending to emergencies across the region. Despite our best efforts, we found ourselves low on the priority list for immediate external assistance.

In the face of this adversity, the school's staff displayed extraordinary initiative and community spirit. Donning work clothes and equipped with whatever tools they had, teachers, administrative staff, and even some parents, who volunteered to help, gathered at the school. It was a remarkable sight: a community united, not just in spirit but in action, to restore their beloved school. The risk and compliance manager in partnership with the property manager and our cleaning contractors took oversight of safety plans to support the voluntary cleanup.

Being abroad I delegated the responsibility and authority to my trusted deputy principal and the executive leadership group. I was available but was not called upon, thanks to the competencies and confidence of the executive team and the systems we had in place.

Reopening and reflections

The cleanup was a laborious and time-consuming process. Over the next three days, the staff worked tirelessly, clearing debris, making temporary repairs, and ensuring the school was safe for students to return. Their dedication was a testament to their commitment to the school and the community it served.

Reopening the school was a moment of triumph mixed with relief. It was not just about resuming academic activities; it was a celebration of resilience, a testament to what can be achieved when a community comes together in the face of adversity. The reopening was marked by a special assembly, where students and staff reflected on the events, shared their experiences, and expressed gratitude to everyone who contributed to the recovery efforts.

The storm and its aftermath brought several critical lessons to the forefront. The school recognised the need for a more robust disaster response plan, including regular safety drills and emergency preparedness training for staff and students. It also highlighted the importance of having a contingency fund for unforeseen events and the necessity of regular maintenance and assessment of the school's infrastructure and natural surroundings.

Failure is part of the learning process

In the journey of leadership, not all risks result in rewards, and not all visions come to fruition as planned. It's crucial for leaders to recognise that failure, while difficult, is often an integral part of the learning process. Being kind to oneself in times of failure is not just about self-preservation; it's about cultivating resilience and the capacity to move forward with grace and wisdom.

An effective leader must balance the drive for success with an acceptance that not every gamble will pay off. The story of a principal at a Jewish school in Sydney, where a major initiative failed dramatically, serves as a poignant reminder of the harsh realities of leadership. That failure cost the principal their job. It highlights the need for leaders to be prepared for potential backlash and to have strategies in place for managing personal and organisational stress when plans go awry.

Leaders should foster a culture where failure is seen not as a catastrophe but as a stepping stone to greater understanding and eventual success. This involves setting realistic expectations, within both themselves and their teams, and promoting an environment where constructive feedback and honest reflection are valued over blame. Self-compassion should be a cornerstone of this approach, encouraging leaders to treat themselves with the same empathy and understanding they offer others.

Furthermore, in the event that an initiative does fail, a wise leader reflects on what went wrong, gleans insights from the experience, and communicates openly with their team about the lessons learned. This not only helps in salvaging and redirecting the efforts but also strengthens the trust and morale within the team.

Effective leadership includes the ability to navigate the dual realities of potential success and possible failure. Leaders must equip themselves with the emotional and strategic tools to manage both outcomes. The real measure of a leader's mettle is often not how they celebrate success, but how they handle failure: not with self-reproach or despondency, but with thoughtful analysis, a resilient spirit, and a readiness to adapt and persevere.

8.4 Handling security threats – the escaped paedophile incident

Our peaceful routine was abruptly disrupted by news that would send any school on high alert. An escaped paedophile, previously incarcerated in the nearby local jail, was reportedly seen in the vicinity of our school. The immediacy and severity of this threat posed an unprecedented challenge to our school's security protocols and our ability to ensure the safety of our students and staff.

Upon receiving this alarming information – not from the police but through local community channels – we had to act swiftly and decisively. The decision to go into lockdown was made without hesitation. Our primary objective was to safeguard every person on our campus.

The lockdown procedure was initiated precisely, a testament to our regular drills and the staff's familiarity with emergency protocols. All exterior doors were secured, and students were gathered in predetermined safe areas. Teachers trained for such scenarios maintained a calm demeanour, focusing on keeping the students composed and comfortable.

Communication with law enforcement was our next crucial step. However, our attempts to gain more information and assistance from the police were met with a notable lack of urgency. The local area commander assured us that there was no direct threat to the school, a statement that stood in stark contrast to the concerns of our immediate community. He said to me: "If there was a threat to your school, I would contact you."

Meanwhile, news of the incident and our lockdown spread rapidly among parents, causing understandable alarm and anxiety. Parents, some bordering on hysteria, flooded our phone lines seeking reassurance about their children's safety. No parents came to the school, however, to collect their children, trusting in the school's leadership.

Resolution and debriefing

The situation reached its resolution when the police apprehended the individual later that day, thankfully without any incident at or near our school. However, the ordeal was far from over. The aftermath required careful handling, particularly in addressing the concerns of our parent community and reviewing our response to the crisis.

In the days following, we organised (virtual) meetings with parents to discuss the incident. Transparency was our guiding principle. We explained the steps taken during the lockdown and our interactions with law enforcement and addressed their concerns. Recognising the emotional impact of the incident, we provided access to counselling services for students, staff, and parents.

The debrief with our staff was a crucial component of our post-incident review. Despite the police's reassurance, our team maintained composure, reflecting their trust in our crisis management capabilities honed through past experiences. We dissected every aspect of our response – from the lockdown initiation to communication with parents and coordination with law enforcement. This comprehensive review helped us identify areas for improvement, particularly in strengthening our external communication channels and protocols for such security threats.

In these situations you have to manage a delicate balance between the varying sources of information. The police are guarded and restricted in the information they can provide, while the community "billboard" runs freely with information, some reliable and a lot not!

In conclusion, the escaped paedophile incident, while deeply unsettling, provided significant insights into crisis management, particularly in handling security threats. The experience reinforced the need for preparedness, effective communication, and strong leadership, ensuring the school remains a safe haven for all its members.

8.5 Lessons from crisis management scenarios

Reflecting on the three real-life crisis scenarios – the unprecedented flood, the devastating storm, and the security threat posed by an escaped paedophile – several key lessons emerge. These diverse scenarios collectively emphasise the critical importance of preparedness, adaptability, and strong leadership in navigating crisis situations in schools.

1. **Importance of emergency preparedness.** Each crisis highlighted the essential need for emergency preparedness. Schools must have well-rehearsed plans for a range of potential emergencies, ensuring swift and coordinated responses that prioritise the safety and well-being of students and staff.
2. **Adaptability in the face of unpredictability.** Crises are inherently unpredictable. The ability to adapt to rapidly changing situations, as seen in the flood and storm incidents, is crucial. School leaders must be able to make quick decisions based on the available information and adjust plans as new challenges arise.
3. **Strong and calm leadership.** In all scenarios, the common denominator for effective crisis management was strong and composed leadership. Leaders must be able to maintain a calm presence, instilling confidence and stability among staff and students, and guiding the school community through the turmoil.
4. **Effective communication.** Clear and timely communication is vital during a crisis. Whether it's keeping the school community informed during a lockdown, liaising with emergency services, or addressing parental concerns post-crisis, effective communication helps manage the situation more efficiently and reduces panic and misinformation.

5. **Community and teamwork.** Crises often unite communities, as seen in the collective cleanup efforts post-storm. Encouraging a sense of community and teamwork aids not only in the immediate response but also in the recovery and healing process.
6. **Continuous learning and improvement.** Post-crisis evaluations are invaluable. They provide insights into what worked well and what needs improvement. This ongoing learning and development in crisis management is crucial for enhancing the school's resilience and preparedness for future emergencies.
7. **Emotional support and psychological safety.** Addressing the psychological impact of crises on students, staff, and parents is as important as addressing physical safety. Providing support and counselling services post-crisis is essential for the emotional well-being of the school community.
8. **Building relationships with external agencies.** Establishing and maintaining strong relationships with local authorities and emergency services is vital. These relationships can be crucial during a crisis, as seen in the handling of the security threat scenario. I did have the local area commander's mobile phone number in my phone contacts.

8.6 Reflections from the Covid-19 pandemic

The Covid-19 pandemic, a global crisis of unprecedented scale, has reshaped the landscape of education and leadership in profound ways. As principals, we found ourselves navigating uncharted territories, forced to adapt and reinvent our approaches to education swiftly. I did discuss the pandemic in Chapter 6 through a different lens: effective communications. This subchapter explores the critical lessons learned from the pandemic, highlighting the resilience, adaptability, and innovation that emerged from this challenging period.

1. **Embracing flexibility and adaptability.** One of the most significant lessons from the pandemic was the importance of flexibility and adaptability in leadership. The rapid shift to remote learning demanded quick decision-making and a departure from traditional educational models. As principals, we learned to be more agile, adapting our strategies to meet the evolving needs of our students and staff. This adaptability extended beyond academic delivery to

encompass all aspects of school life, including student welfare, staff support, and community engagement.

2. **Importance of effective communication.** The pandemic accentuated the crucial role of clear, consistent, and compassionate communication. With information and guidelines changing rapidly, principals had to ensure that all stakeholders – students, teachers, parents, and the broader community – were kept informed and reassured. We learned the value of utilising various communication channels and the power of transparent communication in building trust and maintaining a sense of community, even in a virtual environment.

3. **Fostering resilience and well-being.** The emotional and psychological impact of the pandemic on students and staff brought the issue of mental health to the forefront. As leaders, we recognise the need to foster academic and emotional resilience. We learned to prioritise well-being, integrating mental health support into our educational frameworks. This crisis taught us to be more empathetic leaders, attentive to the well-being of our school community and proactive in providing support and resources.

4. **Leveraging technology in education.** The pandemic accelerated the integration of technology in education. Necessity led to innovation, with schools rapidly adopting new technologies for remote learning. As principals, we learned the importance of digital literacy, for both ourselves and our staff. We saw the potential of technology in enhancing educational delivery, offering personalised learning experiences, and ensuring continuity of education regardless of physical constraints.

5. **Reinforcing the value of community and collaboration.** The pandemic highlighted the strength of community and the power of collaboration. It brought schools, families, and local communities closer together, working in unison to support each other through the crisis. As principals, we learned the importance of building strong community networks and the benefits of collaborative approaches, both within and outside the school setting.

6. **Preparing for future crises.** Lastly, Covid-19 taught us the importance of crisis preparedness. It emphasised the need for robust contingency plans, flexible policies, and an ethos of continuous learning and improvement. As educational leaders, we now understand more than ever the importance of being prepared for the unexpected, having

adaptable frameworks in place, and cultivating a culture of resilience and innovation.

In conclusion, the Covid-19 pandemic was a defining moment for educational leadership. It challenged us, reshaped our understanding of education, and brought to light the essential qualities of effective leadership in times of crisis. As we move forward, these lessons will continue to guide us, not just in navigating future crises but in shaping a more resilient, adaptive, and innovative educational landscape. The pandemic, while a crisis of monumental proportions, has been a catalyst for growth and learning, leaving an indelible mark on the journey of every principal.

8.7 Security measures like metal detectors for Australian schools

In response to increasing concerns about school security, particularly in environments with significant risk factors such as high local crime rates or specific community threats, the decision to implement measures such as metal detectors should be carefully considered by each school's leadership.

This decision is inherently school-specific, influenced by the school's location, community context, and assessed risks to students and staff. For example, in Australian schools, there is an ongoing debate regarding the use of metal detectors (Duffin, 2024). I support the implementation of such measures if the school's leadership determines there is a credible risk of students bringing weapons to school.

Furthermore, the experience of managing security with the support of the security firms underscores the importance of having a well-defined and practised security protocol. Frequent meetings to develop and workshop multiple scenarios, from "lone wolf" attacks to bomb threats, are crucial. This proactive approach involves establishing a clear chain of command and detailed standard operating procedures (SOP) that are communicated to key personnel, including the board, the internal security group, and selected staff members.

Given these considerations, it is advisable for schools to consider forming a dedicated security committee, potentially as a subset of the existing workplace health and safety (WHS) committee. This specialised committee would focus on tailoring the school's security measures to its specific needs, ensuring preparedness and swift, effective responses to any threats.

8.8 Key takeaways

The success of our initiatives often sprang from the collaborative efforts of our entire team. For instance, when faced with the flood crisis, it was the collective insights and dedicated efforts of our team that steered us to a successful outcome. Each team member brought unique expertise and viewpoints that were crucial in addressing the multifaceted aspects of the challenge, demonstrating the powerful impact of a united leadership approach.

During times of crisis, the role of a collaborative leader shifts subtly from direct command to more of a guiding force, enabling the team to execute well-practised response strategies effectively. This was evident when handling the security crisis, where my role was to support and empower the response team, ensuring they had the resources and autonomy needed to manage the situation effectively. This approach not only expedited our response but also reinforced the trust and capability within our team, highlighting the importance of nurturing leadership at all levels.

CHAPTER 9

THE ETHICAL COMPASS
Ethical decision-making and integrity

9.1 Foundations of integrity

Ethics and integrity form the bedrock of effective educational leadership. At the core of a school leader's role lies the responsibility to not only impart knowledge but also model values that shape young minds. This chapter emphasises the critical importance of ethical decision-making and integrity in educational leadership.

Principals are frequently confronted with situations that challenge their moral compass. These challenges range from handling sensitive information and ensuring fairness in resource allocation to confronting personal biases in disciplinary actions. Each decision a leader makes can have far-reaching implications for the school community, making it imperative to navigate these situations with a keen sense of ethics and integrity.

In this chapter, we will explore four distinct ethical dilemmas that educational leaders often encounter:

1. **Confidentiality vs transparency.** We examine a scenario where a teacher is under investigation for misconduct. This situation presents a challenge in balancing the need for confidentiality with the value of transparency within the school community. How do leaders navigate this delicate balance while upholding ethical standards?

2. **Fairness in resource allocation.** This dilemma involves the difficult decision of allocating limited resources. Leaders may find themselves choosing between funding advanced placement programs or enhancing resources for struggling students. How should leaders approach such decisions to ensure fairness and equity for all students?
3. **Addressing unconscious bias in discipline.** Here, I share a scenario where a school leader must confront their unconscious biases in a disciplinary situation involving a student with a history of behavioural issues. This situation tests the leader's ability to remain impartial and fair while dealing with complex disciplinary matters.
4. **Navigating personal relationships in a professional setting.** This ethical dilemma involves a teacher who, because of their close friendship with a parent, is privy to sensitive information about other students and is perceived to give preferential treatment to their friend's child.

Each scenario is accompanied by reflection questions designed to encourage deeper thinking and introspection about navigating these ethical challenges effectively. Through this exploration, the chapter aims to equip educational leaders with the insights and tools necessary to make decisions that are effective, morally sound, and aligned with the principles of integrity.

The journey through these ethical dilemmas is not just about finding immediate solutions but about fostering an enduring commitment to ethical leadership that resonates through every aspect of school management and leadership.

9.2 Balancing transparency and confidentiality

The dilemma of balancing confidentiality with transparency is not uncommon. This delicate balance becomes particularly challenging when a teacher is under investigation for misconduct. This subchapter explores such a scenario, where a school leader must navigate the complex interplay of maintaining confidentiality for the individual involved while upholding the value of transparency within the school community.

The ethical dilemma

Consider a situation where a teacher at your school is under investigation for alleged misconduct. The allegations, if true, could have significant implications for the teacher's career, the students' welfare, and the school's reputation. As a leader, you are privy to sensitive information about the investigation. Simultaneously, there is growing speculation and concern among the school community – staff, students, and parents alike.

The context

In this scenario, the teacher's right to confidentiality must be weighed against the community's right to transparency. Confidentiality is crucial to ensure a fair and unbiased investigation, protect the individuals involved from undue public scrutiny, and maintain the integrity of the investigative process. However, transparency is also important to maintain trust within the school community, ensure that concerns are being addressed, and prevent the spreading of rumours and misinformation.

Reflection questions

1. **Balancing transparency with confidentiality.** How would you balance the need for transparency with the teacher's right to confidentiality? Consider the legal and ethical implications of sharing information about the investigation. How much information should be shared to keep the community informed without compromising the teacher's privacy and the integrity of the investigation?
2. **Factors influencing disclosure.** What factors would influence your decision on what information to disclose? Reflect on aspects such as the severity of the allegations, the stage of the investigation, the legal advice received, and the level of concern within the school community.
3. **Addressing community concerns.** How would you address concerns from parents and staff while respecting confidentiality? Think about strategies for communicating with different stakeholders, managing their expectations, and reassuring them about the school's commitment to safety and fairness without divulging sensitive details.

This ethical dilemma requires a nuanced approach, balancing the legal and moral obligations towards the teacher under investigation and the needs of the broader school community. Navigating this scenario effectively calls for a deep understanding of ethical principles, strong communication skills, and a commitment to upholding the values of fairness and integrity. In most jurisdictions in Australia, the process to be followed is mandated by state bodies such as the Office of Children's Guardian in NSW – any response by you as the principal has to be within the mandatory reporting requirements.

9.3 Fairness in resource allocation

One of the most challenging aspects of educational leadership is the equitable allocation of limited resources. This subchapter examines a dilemma faced by many school leaders: choosing between funding an advanced placement (AP) program that benefits high-achieving students or diverting those resources to improve support for struggling students. This decision involves practical considerations and a deep dive into the ethical principles of fairness and equity in education.

The ethical dilemma

Imagine your school has a limited budget for new initiatives or additional resources. You are faced with a choice: allocate this budget to an advanced placement program, which offers enriched academic opportunities for high-achieving students, or use the funds to bolster resources for struggling students. The former can enhance the school's academic reputation and provide exceptional opportunities for some students. At the same time, the latter could improve overall educational outcomes and support for those who might be falling behind.

The context

This scenario is a test of balancing competing educational priorities. On one hand, the AP program could provide high-achieving students with the challenges and opportunities they need to excel further. On the other hand, allocating resources to struggling students could significantly improve their academic performance and self-esteem, potentially closing the achievement gap. This decision has far-reaching implications for student equity, academic performance, and the overall educational environment of the school.

Reflection questions

1. **Assessing needs and impact.** How would you assess the needs and impact of resource allocation on different student groups? Consider the short-term and long-term academic and social implications for high-achieving and struggling students. How do you weigh the benefits of providing advanced opportunities against the needs of those requiring additional support?
2. **Guiding ethical principles.** What ethical principles would guide your decision-making in this scenario? Reflect on the concepts of equity,

equality, and justice in education. How do you define what is fair and equitable in the context of diverse student needs?

3. **Mitigating negative impacts.** How might you mitigate any negative impacts of your decision? If you choose one option over the other, how can you address potential feelings of neglect or unfairness in the group not receiving the new resources? Could alternative strategies or compromises be employed to support both groups?

Navigating this dilemma requires a thoughtful and balanced approach, considering the diverse needs of the student population, the ethical implications of the decision, and the potential long-term impacts on the school community. This scenario challenges school leaders to think critically about using limited resources to foster an inclusive and supportive educational environment.

9.4 Addressing personal bias in discipline matters

One of the most subtle yet significant challenges is the influence of personal biases, particularly in disciplinary situations. This subchapter explores a scenario where a school leader must navigate their unconscious biases while handling a disciplinary case involving a student with a history of behavioural issues. Such situations demand high self-awareness and ethical consideration to ensure fairness and justice.

The ethical dilemma

Consider a situation where a student, known for previous behavioural issues, is involved in a new disciplinary case. As a leader, you know the student's history, which may unconsciously influence your perception and judgment in the current situation. The dilemma lies in recognising and managing these biases to ensure a fair and impartial disciplinary process. How you handle this case can have significant implications for the student's future at the school and their perception of justice and fairness.

The context

This scenario tests your ability to separate past knowledge from present circumstances. It challenges you to consider how your perceptions, potentially coloured by the student's history, might impact your judgment. The situation calls for a careful, balanced approach that respects the student's rights while upholding the school's disciplinary standards.

Reflection questions

1. **Mitigating personal bias.** What steps would you take to ensure your personal biases do not affect your judgment in this disciplinary case? Consider strategies such as consulting with unbiased colleagues, reviewing similar past cases for consistency, or even seeking external advice to gain different perspectives.
2. **Ensuring fairness and impartiality.** How would you ensure a fair and impartial process for all students involved, including those with a history of behavioural issues? Reflect on the importance of following established disciplinary procedures, ensuring that all students are given an equal opportunity to present their side of the story, and making decisions based on facts and evidence rather than assumptions or past experiences.
3. **Role of reflection and self-awareness.** What is the role of reflection and self-awareness in making ethical decisions in such cases? Think about how regular self-reflection on decision-making processes and biases can help you become a more ethical and fair leader. How can ongoing professional development and training in areas such as equity, diversity, and inclusion support you in this process?

Addressing personal bias in discipline matters is crucial for ethical leadership in education. It requires a commitment to self-examination, a dedication to fairness, and a continuous effort to understand and mitigate the influence of unconscious biases. This scenario emphasises the need for leaders to be vigilant about their internal processes and committed to upholding the highest standards of equity and justice in their schools.

9.5 Navigating personal relationships in a professional setting

The dilemma of managing personal relationships within a professional context is both challenging and prevalent. This becomes particularly complex when teachers form close friendships with parents of students. This subchapter digs into such a scenario, where a school leader must navigate the fine line between personal and professional boundaries, ensuring fairness and impartiality in a setting where personal relationships could lead to conflicts of interest or perceptions of favouritism.

The ethical dilemma

Imagine a situation where a teacher at your school has developed a close personal friendship with a parent. This friendship extends beyond the school, involving social gatherings and shared personal interests. The teacher, through their relationship with the parent, becomes privy to sensitive information about other students or is perceived to show preferential treatment towards their friend's child. This situation raises significant ethical concerns about fairness, professionalism, and the maintenance of an unbiased educational environment.

The context

In this scenario, the need to maintain professional boundaries and prevent any conflict of interest must be weighed against respecting personal relationships. The teacher's friendship with a parent can lead to perceptions of unfairness among other students and parents, potentially impacting the teacher's objectivity and the trust placed in them by the school community. However, it is also important to acknowledge the right of staff to engage in personal relationships outside of their professional responsibilities.

Reflection questions

1. **Maintaining professional boundaries.** How would you address the issue of a teacher's close friendship with a parent to ensure professional boundaries are maintained? Consider the implications this friendship could have on the teacher's objectivity and the perception of other students and parents.
2. **Strategies for managing perceptions of favouritism.** What strategies could be implemented to manage and mitigate perceptions of favouritism or conflict of interest arising from such relationships? Reflect on how you would communicate these strategies to your staff and the school community.
3. **Balancing personal and professional lives.** How would you guide your staff in balancing their personal and professional lives, especially in contexts where these overlap? Consider the role of school policies in guiding such situations.
4. **Handling sensitive information.** If a teacher is privy to sensitive information through their personal relationship with a parent, how would you ensure that this information is handled appropriately and does not influence professional duties?

This ethical dilemma requires a careful and thoughtful approach, balancing respect for personal relationships with the need to uphold professionalism and trust in the educational environment. It calls for a nuanced understanding of ethical principles, effective communication, and the enforcement of clear boundaries and policies within the school setting.

9.6 Key takeaways

As presented in this chapter, the exploration of ethical dilemmas in educational leadership underscores the intricate and often challenging nature of ethical decision-making and integrity in the field. The scenarios discussed – balancing transparency and confidentiality, ensuring fairness in resource allocation, confronting personal bias in disciplinary matters, and navigating personal relationships in a professional setting – highlight the multifaceted aspects of ethical leadership. These examples illustrate that ethical decision-making extends beyond straightforward choices; it often involves navigating complex situations where values, principles, and practical considerations intersect.

One of the critical insights from this chapter is the importance of ongoing self-reflection in ethical decision-making. Leaders must continuously examine their biases and motivations and the impact of their decisions on the school community. This introspective process is vital in maintaining integrity and ensuring that decisions align with both personal and professional ethical standards.

Moreover, a commitment to ethical principles in educational leadership is fundamental. It involves consistently applying values such as fairness, transparency, justice, and respect in every aspect of leadership. This commitment not only guides leaders through challenging situations but also serves as a model for the entire school community, fostering an environment where ethical considerations are deeply ingrained in the culture.

In conclusion, the journey through ethical dilemmas is a continuous learning process for educational leaders. It requires a balance of self-awareness, principled decision-making, and an unwavering commitment to do what is right, even in the face of complexity and uncertainty. By embracing these challenges and reflecting on the ethical dimensions of their roles, leaders can navigate their responsibilities with integrity, setting a powerful example for the entire educational community.

CHAPTER 10

ACHIEVING WORK-LIFE HARMONY AS A PRINCIPAL

10.1 Crafting balance in leadership

The role of a principal is undeniably rewarding, yet it comes with a set of challenges that can stretch the boundaries of personal and professional life. Striking a balance between the demanding responsibilities of school leadership and personal well-being is desirable and essential for long-term effectiveness and fulfilment. This chapter explores the pursuit of work-life harmony, a crucial aspect often overshadowed in the discourse on educational leadership.

In a school's dynamic and fast-paced environment, principals often find themselves juggling numerous tasks, addressing immediate concerns, and planning for the future, all while being the linchpin of their educational communities. The intensity of these responsibilities can encroach on personal time, making it challenging to maintain a healthy balance. Recognising and addressing this imbalance is critical, not just for the health and well-being of the principals themselves but also for the overall health of the school community they lead.

One valuable strategy I depended on to achieve this harmony was to embrace a structured start to my day. A 5 a.m. start worked for me, dedicated to a walk, quiet reflective time, a coffee to launch the new day, and a purposeful, consistent routine allowing me to arrive at work ready to fire. This early morning ritual serves as a grounding exercise, providing a sense of control and tranquillity before the day's demands set in. It energises the mind and body, setting a positive tone for the day ahead.

This chapter offers practical advice and strategies to help principals navigate the complexities of their roles while maintaining personal well-being. It underscores the importance of setting boundaries, prioritising self-care, and finding routines that rejuvenate and empower. Achieving work–life harmony is not about dividing time equally between work and personal life but about finding a rhythm that sustains your enthusiasm and passion both as a leader and as an individual.

10.2 The balancing act – work and personal life

For school principals, the juggling act between professional duties and personal life is more than mere preference – it is a critical necessity. The relentless demands of the role make it imperative to strike a healthy balance, not only to sustain the energy and focus needed for effective leadership but also to maintain the passion for education.

The importance of a balanced life

A principal's responsibilities rarely end with the school bell. These obligations can stretch into evenings and weekends, infringing upon personal time. This encroachment can lead to burnout, diminished job satisfaction, and adverse effects on personal relationships and health. It is crucial for principals to understand that prioritising their well-being is not an act of selfishness but a strategic necessity for maintaining their effectiveness as leaders.

A well-balanced life provides the opportunity for principals to disconnect, recharge, and gain fresh perspectives, enabling them to return to their roles with enhanced vigour and clarity.

Family life can be a principal's stronghold, offering emotional support and stability amidst the chaos of educational leadership. However, the intensity of the job can sometimes overshadow family commitments, leading to strained relationships and personal dissatisfaction. To cultivate a healthier balance, principals might consider implementing these practices; they worked for me.

- **Scheduled family time.** Just as they schedule school meetings and responsibilities, principals should carve out non-negotiable time for family activities. Whether it's a weekly dinner date, weekend outings,

or evening walks, these scheduled moments can help maintain strong family bonds.
- **Open communication.** Regularly communicate with family members about the demands of your job and the potential for unexpected responsibilities. This openness can foster understanding and support from family members, who can become allies in finding balance.
- **Creating boundaries.** Establish clear boundaries between work and home. This might involve setting specific times when work calls and emails are off-limits or having a dedicated workspace that doesn't encroach on communal family areas.

Guidance on leaving work at work

Disconnecting from work responsibilities when at home is essential for maintaining personal well-being and nurturing family relationships. Here are some strategies that I employed.

- **Physical and digital separation.** Physically leave work materials at the office and use digital tools like email filters to manage the influx of communications after hours. Establishing a ritual to end the work day, such as a recap of the day's achievements and a to-do list for tomorrow, can also signal to your brain that work has ended.
- **Professional support networks.** Build a network of fellow principals and educators who understand the challenges of the role. This community can provide emotional support, share strategies for balancing life, and offer a forum for venting frustrations outside the family sphere.
- **Delegate and empower.** One of the effective ways to manage workload is to delegate tasks appropriately within the school's staff. This not only reduces your workload but also empowers others by showing trust in their capabilities, fostering a more collaborative environment.
- **Professional development focused on work–life balance.** Invest in training that offers strategies for time management, delegation, and stress reduction. These skills are crucial for maintaining a boundary between personal and professional life.

By embedding these practices into daily routines, principals can safeguard their personal time, ensuring that their professional responsibilities enhance rather than detract from their family life and personal well-being. This balance is not only beneficial for the principals themselves but also sets a positive example for staff and students about the importance of work–life harmony.

Strategies for setting boundaries

One key strategy that has been instrumental in my own life as a principal is setting clear boundaries around what constitutes a work day and a work week. Here are some ways to implement this strategy:

1. **Define work hours.** Establish clear start and end times for your work day. Communicate these hours to your staff and colleagues to set expectations regarding your availability.
2. **Prioritise tasks.** Not all tasks are of equal importance. Prioritise your workload to focus on what needs to be done during your defined work hours. This helps prevent work from spilling into your personal time.
3. **Use technology wisely.** Technology can be both a boon and a bane. Set specific times to check emails or messages outside of work hours, if necessary, and avoid the temptation to be constantly connected.
4. **Delegate effectively.** Delegation is a key leadership skill. Trust your team with responsibilities, which will lighten your workload and empower them.
5. **Schedule personal time.** Just as you schedule meetings and work tasks, schedule time for family, hobbies, and self-care. Treat this time as a non-negotiable appointment with yourself.
6. **Learn to say no.** Recognising that you cannot do everything is important. Saying no to certain demands or requests is crucial in maintaining your boundaries.
7. **Have regular check-ins with self.** Regularly assess how well you maintain your work–life balance. Be open to adjusting your strategies as needed.

Maintaining a balance between work and personal life is critical for the well-being and effectiveness of a school principal. It requires setting clear boundaries, prioritising tasks, and being mindful of one's own needs. By implementing these strategies, principals can ensure they give their best to their schools while caring for themselves.

It is important in this subchapter to address a sensitive yet crucial topic: the role of **alcohol** in the lives of busy executives. Often, in the high-pressure world of executive leadership, alcohol can subtly shift from being a social lubricant to being a habitual form of stress relief. This transition, largely unspoken, becomes the proverbial elephant in the room. It is a social ailment that, while common, is seldom discussed openly in professional circles.

Excessive reliance on alcohol may not only undermine personal health and well-being but also impact decision-making and leadership effectiveness. Acknowledging this issue is not about casting judgment but fostering awareness. It is essential for leaders to recognise the importance of moderation and the value of seeking healthier, more sustainable methods of stress management. This awareness is a critical component of self-care and maintaining the mental clarity and emotional resilience necessary for effective leadership.

10.3 Personal organisation and energy management

In the demanding role of a school principal, personal organisation and energy management are not just skills – they are essential survival tools. This subchapter discusses practical techniques for enhancing productivity and reducing stress, focusing on controlling your diary, taking meaningful breaks, and ensuring a balanced mix of work and reflective time within each day.

Control your diary

Taking control of your calendar and schedule is paramount. While it is commonplace for busy executives to delegate the management of their diaries to executive assistants, I advocate for a more hands-on approach. It is crucial for principals to personally oversee their scheduling, ensuring a balance between professional commitments and personal well-being.

Granting executive assistants read-only access to your diary fosters a collaborative approach, where they remain informed and can assist effectively. However, you, as the principal, should retain the ultimate control, carving out and protecting essential free time and slots available for appointments. This practice not only ensures a well-balanced schedule that aligns with personal priorities and professional objectives but also empowers you to stay grounded and focused.

By managing your own calendar, you can make strategic decisions about your time, an invaluable asset, and maintain a sense of control and personal agency in your hectic professional life.

The first step towards effective personal organisation is gaining control over your diary. This means being proactive in scheduling and guarding your time. Here are some tips:

- **Plan ahead.** At the start of each week, review your schedule. Prioritise tasks and allocate specific time slots for them in your diary.
- **Limit open access.** While it is important to be approachable, constant interruptions can disrupt your workflow. Set specific "open door" hours for staff and students.
- **Include buffer time.** Always include buffer time between meetings and tasks. This allows you to prepare, reflect, or simply catch your breath. I would schedule 50-minute meetings and set aside an hour in my diary, for example. The attendee would know the meeting was only 50 minutes. I would try to avoid scheduling back-to-back meetings.
- **Say no when necessary.** You don't have to attend every meeting or event. Assess the value and relevance of requests against your priorities.

Taking meaningful breaks

Breaks are not just pauses in your day; they are opportunities to rejuvenate and boost productivity.

- **Schedule breaks.** Integrate short, regular breaks into your daily schedule. Use this time to step away from your desk, stretch, or take a brief walk.
- **Prioritise quality over quantity.** A 10-minute break spent mindfully is more refreshing than an hour spent scrolling through emails.
- **Disconnect to reconnect.** During breaks, disconnect from work-related thoughts. Engage in activities that relax your mind, like reading, meditating, or a quick chat with a colleague about non-work topics.

Balancing work and thinking time

A well-structured day should include a mix of active work and reflective thinking.

- **Allocate time for reflection.** Block out time in your diary for strategic thinking and planning. Use this time to reflect on long-term goals, challenges, and innovations.
- **Diversify your tasks.** Avoid packing your day with only one type of task. Balance meetings, administrative work, and strategic planning throughout the day.

- **Finish with an end-of-day review.** Spend the last 15 minutes of your day reviewing what you've accomplished and planning for the next day. This helps in closing the day's work mentally and preparing for the next.

Managing your personal organisation and energy effectively is about more than just time management; it is about making conscious choices on how to best utilise your time and energy. By controlling your diary, taking meaningful breaks, and ensuring a balanced mix of work and reflective time, you can enhance your productivity while maintaining your well-being. As a principal, these practices will not only benefit you personally but will also set a positive example for your staff and students.

10.4 Cultivating resilience and mental toughness

Resilience and mental toughness are not just desirable traits; they are essential for navigating the myriad challenges that come with the role. This subchapter explores the importance of these qualities in a school leader's repertoire and offers practical advice on developing them. It is told through the lens of my personal experience, where I consciously chose to face challenges head-on as a means of building my resilience and mental toughness.

Embracing challenges to build resilience

Early in my career as a school leader, I recognised the importance of being resilient and mentally tough. However, understanding these qualities and actually possessing them are two different things. I realised that if I were to develop these traits, I had to step out of my comfort zone. Therefore, I adopted a practice that, while unconventional, proved to be immensely effective – I began to purposefully insert myself into challenging situations.

Instead of steering clear of difficult or uncomfortable scenarios, I chose to walk toward them. This approach was not born out of a desire to be confrontational or brazen; rather, it was a calculated strategy to build my capacity to handle adversity. Whether it was addressing conflicts among staff, managing tough conversations with parents, or navigating complex administrative challenges, I saw each of these situations as an opportunity to grow.

The role of resilience and mental toughness

In educational leadership, resilience is about more than enduring tough times; it is about learning from these experiences and emerging stronger. Mental toughness complements this by providing the fortitude to make difficult decisions and stand firm in the face of criticism or opposition.

Developing resilience and mental toughness

- **Self-reflection.** Regular self-reflection was crucial in this process. Post-confrontation, I would assess my responses, identify what I could have done better, and plan how to apply these insights in the future.
- **Seeking professional support.** I did not hesitate to seek advice and guidance from more experienced colleagues and mentors. Their insights and support were invaluable in helping me navigate complex situations.
- **Use of the school's Employee Assistance Program (EAP).** This is a confidential workplace service that schools provide to their employees to support their well-being in the workplace and in their personal lives. Typically funded entirely by the employer, EAPs are intended to help employees deal with personal or work-related issues that might adversely impact their job performance, health, and mental and emotional well-being.
- **Stress management techniques.** I adopted various stress management techniques, such as stillness and physical exercise, to maintain a clear mind and healthy body. This was essential in keeping my stress levels in check, even when facing challenging scenarios.
- **Embracing learning opportunities.** Each challenging situation was viewed as a learning opportunity. This mindset shift was pivotal in transforming potentially negative experiences into positive growth.
- **My parents.** I know that growing up in western Queensland with parents who had a tough, no-nonsense attitude to life in general gave me broad shoulders and a steely resolve.

Cultivating resilience and mental toughness in educational leadership is a deliberate and ongoing process. It involves facing challenges head-on, reflecting on these experiences, seeking support, and managing stress effectively. By doing so, school leaders can develop the strength and stability needed to lead their schools effectively, no matter what challenges come their way.

10.5 Balancing accessibility with boundaries

The dual challenge of being an approachable leader while also setting healthy personal boundaries is a delicate balancing act for any principal. In this subchapter, I reflect on my experiences with an open-door policy and explore the nuances of maintaining accessibility without compromising personal boundaries and well-being.

The effective open-door policy

During my time as a principal, I firmly believed in the value of being accessible to my school community. To me, an open-door policy was more than just a literal open door to my office; it symbolised my approachability and availability to students, staff, and parents. This policy was effective and well-received, but it required more than just an open door – it demanded discipline, a clear vision, and a deep understanding of my role within the school.

Being accessible meant that people in my school community did not have to wait for a reply to an email or schedule an appointment weeks in advance to speak with me. Whether it was a staff member needing guidance, a student seeking advice, or a parent with a concern, I made it a priority to be available and attentive to their needs. This approach helped in building trust and a sense of connectedness within the school community.

Setting boundaries

However, maintaining this level of accessibility came with its challenges. It was crucial to set boundaries to ensure that my personal time and well-being were also respected. Here is how I managed this balance:

- **Defined availability hours.** While my door was generally open, I established specific hours for drop-in visits. This helped manage my time more effectively and allowed me to dedicate certain periods to uninterrupted work. My calendar was shared with my executive assistant so they had visibility about my commitments.
- **Effective communication.** I communicated my availability clearly to the school community. This transparency helped manage expectations regarding when I could be approached and when I was off-limits.
- **Delegation and trust.** Trusting my team to handle certain issues was key. Delegation allowed me to maintain accessibility without being overwhelmed, and it empowered my staff by showing trust in their capabilities.

- **Prioritising tasks.** Each day, I prioritised tasks to ensure that urgent matters were addressed promptly, while also making time for strategic planning and personal reflection.
- **Self-care routines.** I incorporated self-care routines into my daily schedule. This included short breaks during the day and time for hobbies and family outside of school hours.

Striking a balance between being an accessible principal and setting personal boundaries is essential for effective school leadership. An open-door policy can foster a positive school culture and strong relationships within the community. However, it is equally important to establish boundaries to protect personal time and well-being. This balance is not only beneficial for the principal but also sets a positive example for the entire school community on the importance of respect and self-care.

10.6 Realistic expectations for event attendance

One of the joys and challenges of being a principal is being part of the school's vibrant community life, which often extends beyond the classroom into various events and extracurricular activities. However, managing expectations for attendance at these functions while fulfilling other responsibilities requires a strategic approach. This subchapter discusses setting realistic expectations for event attendance and maintaining a meaningful presence at school functions without over-committing.

Balancing presence and responsibilities

During my time as a principal, I committed to attending as many school events as possible. My approach was not just to be present but to be actively engaged. Whether it was a sports event, a drama production, or a parent–teacher meeting, I tried to ensure that my attendance was meaningful to both myself and the attendees.

However, the reality of the principal's workload means that attending every event is not feasible. On occasions when I couldn't be present, I made sure to delegate attendance to my deputy or another senior staff member. It was important to communicate this to the event organisers and participants, often with an apology for my absence. This approach not only demonstrated my commitment to the school community but also empowered other staff members by entrusting them with representing the school leadership.

Setting realistic expectations

- **Prioritise key events.** Identify and prioritise events that are crucial for your presence, such as major school functions, award ceremonies, and events where your participation adds significant value.
- **Delegate when necessary.** Empower your leadership team to represent you at events you cannot attend. This not only shares the responsibility but also highlights the collective nature of school leadership.
- **Communicate your attendance plans.** Clearly communicate to staff, students, and parents which events you will attend. When you can't attend, explain why and who will attend in your stead.
- **Ensure active participation.** When attending events, ensure active and meaningful participation. Engage with students, staff, and parents; your active presence can have a profound impact.
- **Balance with other responsibilities.** Regularly review your schedule to ensure a balance between event attendance and other critical duties. Be mindful of not letting event attendance overshadow other essential responsibilities.
- **Use technology.** For events you cannot attend in person, consider sending a video message or arranging for a virtual presence. This shows your interest and involvement despite your physical absence.

Scenario – balancing competing events and interests

On a crisp autumn evening, the air at the school was thick with excitement and anticipation. It was a night of significant events, each marking a pinnacle of effort and dedication.

After months of rigorous preparation and intellectual duels, the senior debating team reached the semi-finals of the prestigious state debating competition.

Meanwhile, the school's esteemed string orchestra was poised to grace the concert hall as the opening act for the state orchestra's grand concert night, a rare honour and a testament to their exceptional talent.

Adding to the evening's competitive spirit, the open netball team was gearing up for the state final of the knockout cup, a culmination of their teamwork and athletic prowess.

Amidst this was also a personal milestone – my son's 14th birthday – a special day I promised to celebrate with him. Each event held its own significance, presenting a dilemma of choice and presence.

Reflection questions for the reader

- **Prioritisation of commitments.** How would you prioritise your attendance at these events? What factors would influence your decision to choose one event over the others?
- **Managing personal and professional boundaries.** How do you balance personal commitments with professional responsibilities, especially when they coincide on the same day?
- **Delegation and trust.** In situations where you cannot be present, how do you delegate responsibilities to ensure that all important events are adequately supported?
- **Reflecting on missed moments.** If you had to miss an important personal event like your child's birthday, how would you address this with your family to maintain a healthy work-life balance and show your commitment to your family life?

This scenario and the accompanying questions invite the reader to ponder the complexities of leadership, the challenges of balancing multiple responsibilities, and the art of making difficult decisions while maintaining personal and professional harmony.

Setting realistic expectations for event attendance is about finding a balance. It is about being as present as possible, delegating when necessary, and ensuring that when you do attend, your presence is impactful. As a principal, your visibility at school events is important, but it is equally important to manage this aspect of your role in a way that respects your time and energy and underscores the collaborative nature of school leadership.

What did I choose? I chose my son's birthday and I communicated with each one of the staff on why I could not be present and ensured a delegate attended in my place.

10.7 Mastering effective delegation

Mastering the art of delegation is not just a skill but a necessity. Delegation, when done effectively, not only aids in workload management but also plays a critical role in leadership development, for both the principal and the team. This subchapter explores the nuances of effective delegation through a narrative reflecting my experiences and learnings in this vital area of leadership.

Narrative – the journey to delegating effectively

Like many in leadership positions, I was reluctant to delegate when I first took on the principal role. I had an inherent belief that if I wanted something done right, I had to do it myself. This mindset, however, quickly proved to be unsustainable. The sheer volume of work and the diverse range of responsibilities made it clear that effective delegation was not just an option but a requirement for successful school leadership.

The first step in my journey toward effective delegation was acknowledging its benefits, not just to me but to my entire team. Delegating tasks allowed me to focus on higher-order responsibilities, such as strategic planning and the school's future, while simultaneously providing my team with opportunities for growth and development. It was about trusting their capabilities and supporting them in new challenges.

Identifying tasks to delegate was an exercise in discernment. I learned to evaluate tasks based on their importance, urgency, and the required skill set. Routine administrative tasks, certain types of correspondence, and specific operational responsibilities were identified as delegable. The key was ensuring that these tasks aligned with the strengths and development goals of the staff members they were delegated to.

Choosing the right people for delegation involved understanding their skills, interests, and career aspirations. It was crucial to match the tasks with individuals who not only had the competency to handle them but would also see them as opportunities for learning and growth. This approach turned delegation into a tool for professional development within the school.

Providing adequate support to those I delegated tasks to was essential. This meant being available for guidance, offering resources, and setting clear expectations. Regular check-ins and feedback sessions became a part of the process, ensuring that the delegated tasks were on track and contributing to the individual's development.

Through this journey, I learned that delegation was not about relinquishing control, but was about empowering others. It was about building a team that could function efficiently and cohesively, even in my absence. Effective delegation fostered a sense of ownership and accountability among staff, and it helped cultivate future leaders who were well-equipped to handle the complexities of school leadership.

Mastering the art of effective delegation is a critical skill for any school principal. It requires a balance of trust, discernment, and support. By delegating effectively, principals not only manage their workload more efficiently but also contribute to the growth and development of their team, ultimately strengthening the leadership capacity within the school.

10.8 Key takeaways

As we bring the discussion on achieving work–life harmony as a principal to a close, it is important to reflect on the key strategies that can guide school leaders towards a more balanced and fulfilling professional and personal life. The journey of a principal is demanding and complex, making it crucial to find equilibrium between the responsibilities of leadership and the necessities of personal well-being.

Throughout this exploration, we have analysed various aspects of managing the immense workload of educational leadership while ensuring self-care and personal fulfilment. From controlling your own diary to ensuring that work does not consume every waking hour to taking meaningful breaks that rejuvenate the mind and body, the strategies discussed are designed to help principals navigate their demanding roles more effectively. We have emphasised the importance of being present and active at school events while also setting realistic expectations for such attendance. And crucially, we've explored the art of delegation, which not only aids in workload management but also empowers others and develops future leaders.

The importance of self-care and well-being cannot be overstated. As a principal, your well-being directly impacts your ability to lead effectively. It is essential to prioritise activities that replenish your energy and provide a respite from the demands of your role. This could be through hobbies, spending time with family and friends, or simply allowing yourself moments of solitude and reflection.

However, it is important to recognise that there is no one-size-fits-all solution to achieving work–life harmony. Each principal's situation is unique, influenced by their school context, personal life, and individual preferences. Therefore, continuous self-assessment is crucial. Regularly take stock of your work–life balance:

1. Are the current strategies effective?
2. Do they need tweaking, or is a more significant change required?

Be open to adjusting your methods to find what works best for you in your quest for harmony.

As a principal, you play a pivotal role in shaping the educational experiences of young minds while also managing the intricate workings of a school. Balancing these responsibilities with your personal life is a challenge, but with the right strategies, it is a challenge that can be met with success.

Embrace the practices that enable you to be an effective leader without compromising your personal well-being. Remember, achieving work–life harmony is a continuous process, one that requires commitment, self-awareness, and the courage to make changes for your holistic well-being.

CHAPTER 11

PASSING THE TORCH
Succession planning and leaving a legacy

11.1 Cultivating continuity and legacy

One of the most profound responsibilities a leader shoulders is the preparation for their eventual departure and the subsequent handover of responsibilities. This chapter investigates this crucial yet often overlooked aspect of leadership: preparing for a smooth transition and ensuring that the legacy left behind continues to positively influence the school community.

Succession planning in principalship goes beyond merely selecting a successor. It involves a comprehensive process of identifying and nurturing future leaders, ensuring that the school's vision and values are upheld and that the transition is seamless, maintaining stability and continuity. The importance of this process cannot be overstated. A well-executed succession plan not only safeguards the school's future but also stands as a testament to the foresight and responsibility of the outgoing leader.

Succession planning has become so important as some roles within schools become more specialised. Principals are often appointed by boards to do a specific job: transform school culture; address declining enrolments; weed out recalcitrant staff; take away control of the school from the common room; build parents' trust and confidence in school leadership; and address falling academic standards, to name a few.

Reflecting on my own experiences as a principal, and one in particular that was not from the copybook, I have come to understand the profound impact that leadership transitions can have on a school's culture, performance, and morale. Preparing for leadership succession is not an act that starts at the end of a tenure; it is an ongoing commitment throughout one's leadership journey. It involves recognising and cultivating potential leaders, mentoring them to develop their skills, and ensuring they are ready to take on the mantle when the time comes. It also means making tough decisions, sometimes stepping aside to allow fresh ideas and new energy to lead the way.

In my time, I have faced the challenges of identifying the right individuals who not only possessed the skills but also shared the vision and passion for the school's future. I have learned the importance of open communication with stakeholders during this transition phase – staff, students, parents, and the wider community. Their involvement and acceptance are crucial in legitimising and supporting the new leadership.

On the other hand, leaving a legacy is about the lasting impact one makes – the values instilled, the improvements made, and the vision set forth. It is about ensuring that the foundations laid will support future growth and success. My legacy, I hope, is one that resonates with the values of educational excellence, community building, and continuous improvement.

In principalship, the management of leadership transitions by a school board is a delicate process, fraught with challenges and responsibilities. Reflecting on my own experiences, I recall an instance where a board's approach to succession planning did not align with the school's best interests, students, and the wider community. This situation serves as a poignant reminder of the complexities involved in such transitions and the profound impact they can have on the school's future.

The board in question, though well-intentioned, struggled with a lack of experience and skill in handling the delicate process of leadership transition. Their focus inadvertently shifted towards internal dynamics and concerns rather than the broader needs of the school community. This misalignment resulted in decisions that, though not meant to harm, did not fully consider the implications for the school's continued success and the well-being of its students. It was a situation that highlighted the critical need for boards to have a clear and unified vision, one that transcends individual perspectives and is deeply rooted in the welfare and advancement of the school community.

The sensitive incident underscored the importance of tact, diplomacy, and a strategic approach in managing leadership transitions. It also highlighted the necessity for school boards to have the right skills and understanding to navigate these waters effectively. The experience was a learning opportunity for all involved, emphasising the need for comprehensive planning, open communication, and a steadfast commitment to the school's core values and mission during times of change. It reinforced the idea that at the heart of every decision a school board makes, the primary focus should always be on what is best for the students and the wider community.

As we progress through this chapter, we will explore various facets of succession planning and legacy building. Through personal anecdotes and practical insights, the chapter aims to guide educational leaders on effectively "passing the torch", ensuring that their departure marks not an end but a new beginning for the school and its community.

11.2 Recognising future leaders

During my time as a principal, I worked with many talented leaders, each bringing unique strengths to the table. Among them, a standout was one of my earlier deputies, who joined our school from Queensland Education. His journey from deputy to principal at one of Queensland's most outstanding independent schools over 14 years is a testament to the power of recognising and nurturing leadership potential.

The journey of a future leader

His commitment, insight, and passion for education were immediately evident when my deputy first joined our school. He was naturally able to connect with staff and students, and had a keen understanding of educational leadership and management. However, transitioning from a department role to the leadership dynamics of an independent school required a tailored approach.

Together, we embarked on a journey of professional development and mentorship. We identified key areas for growth and provided opportunities for him to take on leadership roles within the school. This included leading staff development sessions, managing school-wide initiatives, and gradually becoming involved in strategic planning processes. His evolution was a process of mutual learning and adaptation as we worked together to harness his potential and steer it towards the unique demands and opportunities of independent school leadership.

Qualities of effective leaders

Reflecting on this experience, several qualities stand out as indicators of effective leadership potential:

- **Visionary thinking.** The ability to conceptualise and articulate a clear vision for the school's future.
- **Empathy and communication skills.** A strong capacity for empathy, enabling leaders to connect with and inspire their team.
- **Adaptability.** Flexibility and openness to change, crucial in the ever-evolving education landscape.
- **Decision-making ability.** Sound judgment and the ability to make informed decisions, even in complex situations.
- **Commitment to professional growth.** A continuous quest for learning and self-improvement.

Practical advice for fostering potential leaders

- **Provide leadership opportunities.** Offer potential leaders chances to lead projects or initiatives. This not only tests their skills but also builds their confidence.
- **Mentorship and coaching.** Engage in regular one-on-one mentoring. Share experiences, offer guidance, and provide constructive feedback.
- **Encourage professional development.** Support their participation in leadership workshops, conferences, networking, and further education.
- **Foster a culture of leadership.** Create an environment where initiative is encouraged, and successes and learning opportunities are equally valued.
- **Regular check-ins and reflection.** Have regular discussions about their progress, challenges, and aspirations. Encourage reflective practices to foster self-awareness.

Identifying and nurturing future leaders is a pivotal role of current educational leaders. It involves a keen eye for potential, a commitment to mentorship, and creating an environment where leadership can thrive. The journey with my deputy was as enriching for me as it was for him, reminding me that in the process of developing future leaders, we, too, continue to grow and learn.

11.3 The art of mentorship

Mentorship, a crucial component of leadership development, has played a transformative role in my career, especially during my early years as a leader. This subchapter reflects on mentorship's profound impact on my professional journey and explores the intricacies and importance of mentorship in cultivating future leaders.

Mentorship in leadership development can take many forms, from formal mentoring programs to more informal guidance and support. The heart of mentorship lies in the transfer of knowledge, skills, and wisdom from an experienced leader to a less experienced individual. It is about guiding, challenging, and supporting mentees, helping them to navigate the complexities of their roles and encouraging their personal and professional growth.

The influence of a guiding hand

My first principal, a figure I hold in high regard, was instrumental in shaping my approach to leadership. More than assigning leadership positions or responsibilities, he bestowed upon me something far more significant: the gift of autonomy and trust. He allowed me the freedom to lead, make decisions, and learn from both successes and setbacks. This autonomy came with quiet, unwavering support, an assurance that he believed in my capabilities. It was this confidence he had in me that propelled me to strive for excellence and take bold steps in my career. His mentorship was not about hand-holding; it was about empowering me to find my own path, make my own choices, and grow into my own style of leadership.

Practical advice for effective mentorship

- **Practise active listening.** Be an active listener. Understand your mentee's aspirations, challenges, and perspectives. This helps in providing tailored guidance.
- **Foster a safe learning environment.** Create a safe space where mentees feel comfortable sharing their thoughts and concerns. Encourage open and honest communication.
- **Emphasise empowerment over directive.** Focus on empowering rather than directing. Encourage mentees to explore solutions and make decisions, fostering their independence and confidence.

- **Share experiences and insights.** Use your own experiences, both successes and failures, as a learning tool. Sharing your journey can provide valuable insights and inspiration.
- **Encourage reflection.** Encourage mentees to reflect on their experiences. Reflection is a powerful tool for learning and growth.
- **Promote a culture of mentorship.** Foster a school culture where mentorship is valued. Encourage experienced staff to participate in mentorship, creating a supportive and collaborative learning environment.
- **Provide feedback and recognition.** Provide constructive feedback and acknowledge achievements. Recognising progress is crucial in building confidence and motivation.

The art of mentorship is about nurturing potential, guiding professional journeys, and creating a legacy of strong, capable leaders. My experience with my first principal is a testament to a mentor's lasting impact, shaping not just careers but lives. As educational leaders, our role as mentors is not just a responsibility; it is a privilege that can shape the future of education.

11.4 Preparing for transition

School leadership transitions are pivotal events that can shape the school's future trajectory. This subchapter narrates a significant transition in my career – preparing the school for the retirement of a long-serving deputy principal – and the strategies I used for ensuring a smooth transition.

The challenge of replacing a pillar of strength

The retirement of our deputy principal, a stalwart who had served the school for over 15 years, presented a significant challenge. His departure meant losing not just an administrator but a cornerstone of our school's culture. Known for his wisdom, calm demeanour, and exceptional listening skills, he embodied a care and work ethic that was revered by staff, students, and families alike. People who sought his counsel always left his office feeling affirmed, strengthened, and with a clear outcome. The thought of replacing him seemed daunting, almost impossible. His role in the school exceeded his job description; he was a mentor, a confidant, and a guiding force for many.

The importance of preparation for transition

The first step in facing this challenging transition was acknowledging his irreplaceable impact. It was important to manage expectations – no successor would be a carbon copy of him. However, we focused on maintaining what made him an exceptional deputy principal: his approach to leadership and his commitment to the school community.

Practical advice for effective transition planning

- **Early and transparent communication.** We initiated open communication about the impending change well in advance. This transparency helped in managing anxieties and expectations among the school community.
- **Involving stakeholders in the transition.** We involved staff, students, and families in the transition process, recognising their role in shaping the deputy principal's legacy.
- **Identifying key qualities for succession.** We outlined the key qualities and skills the successor would need, focusing on the school's long-term goals and the departing deputy principal's strengths.
- **Comprehensive search and selection process.** The search for a successor was thorough, involving both internal and external candidates, ensuring a wide range of potentials.
- **Structured handover process.** A structured handover plan was developed, which included overlap time for the incoming deputy principal to work alongside the retiring deputy principal.
- **Cultural continuity and change management.** We focused on maintaining cultural continuity while also embracing the fresh perspectives the new deputy principal would bring.
- **Celebrating the legacy.** The school organised a fitting farewell, celebrating the retiring deputy principal's contributions, thereby turning the transition into a celebration of legacy rather than a period of uncertainty.

The transition, while challenging, was an opportunity for growth and renewal. The experience reinforced the idea that effective succession planning is as much about honouring the past as it is about embracing the future. By carefully planning and involving the school community in this process, we ensured a smooth transition, upholding the standards and values that were hallmarks of our retiring deputy principal's tenure.

11.5 Leaving a lasting legacy

The concept of a legacy in school leadership transcends time and tenure. It is about a leader's enduring imprint on a school's culture, ethos, and community. This subchapter reflects on my personal legacy as a school leader and explores the nuances of building a legacy that positively impacts all school stakeholders.

Crafting a legacy of possibility and empathy

At one of the schools I led, my legacy was encapsulated in the belief that "anything was possible". This ethos was not just a motto but a mindset permeating every aspect of school life. It influenced how leaders approached challenges – often asking themselves, "How would Paul handle this?" This question wasn't about emulating my style but rather invoking a problem-solving mindset where all possibilities were explored and solutions were reached collaboratively.

For the students, the legacy was one of empowerment – they knew they could be who they wanted to be with unwavering support from their school and teachers. It was about fostering an environment where every student felt valued and encouraged to pursue their aspirations.

For parents, my leadership provided an empathetic ear and an assurance of standards. It was a balance of understanding and expectation, where parents saw a value proposition – a school that cared deeply for its students while maintaining high standards of education and behaviour.

However, legacies can be fragile, and transitions can be challenging. My successor did not continue in the same vein, choosing instead to light their own torch. This change brought unrest and disorder, starkly contrasting with the previous environment. It is a reminder that while we can lay the foundations and set a direction, the continuity of a legacy is also dependent on those who follow.

Building a lasting, positive legacy

- **Define your core values.** Your legacy should reflect your core values and beliefs. Be clear about what you stand for and ensure these values are evident in your actions and decisions.
- **Foster a culture of collaboration and empowerment.** Create an environment where staff and students feel empowered to take

initiative and voice their ideas. Encourage collaboration and open communication.
- **Be a role model.** Lead by example. Your behaviour and attitude set the tone for the school culture and ethos.
- **Build strong relationships.** Invest time in building relationships with students, staff, and parents. Genuine connections are at the heart of a lasting legacy.
- **Encourage continuous learning and growth.** Promote a continuous improvement and learning culture. Encourage staff and students to pursue their interests and develop their skills.
- **Be adaptable yet consistent.** While being open to change and new ideas, maintain consistency in your principles and how you treat people.

A legacy in educational leadership is about your lasting impact on the school community. It's about creating a positive, empowering environment that endures beyond your tenure. As leaders, our goal should be to leave the school better than we found it, setting a path that others can follow and build upon.

11.6 Embracing the future

Transitioning from one phase of our professional lives to the next is often a journey filled with mixed emotions and critical decisions. This subchapter explores the complexities of moving on from a long-held leadership role, embracing change, and stepping into the future with optimism and purpose.

A turning point in my career

My time at a school where I served as an executive leader for 10 years was a period of profound professional growth and personal fulfilment. However, the retirement of my principal, who had been my mentor and hero for over a decade, marked the beginning of a significant change. The new principal who took over had a different vision and style, and it became clear within the first month that our professional dynamics were not aligning. Realising that I was no longer the right fit for the school I had devoted a significant part of my life to was painful and disconcerting.

The decision to leave was not easy. It meant saying goodbye to a community I loved, to relationships I had nurtured, and to a part of my identity. Yet, it was a necessary step to make way for new opportunities and challenges.

It was a time for reflection, re-evaluating my goals, and rekindling my passion for educational leadership in a new context.

Embracing change and moving forward

- **Acknowledge your emotions.** Recognise and accept the emotions associated with leaving a role – sadness, loss, uncertainty, hope, and excitement for what lies ahead.
- **Reflect on your journey.** Take time to reflect on your achievements, the relationships you've built, and the impact you've had. This reflection is a source of strength and a foundation for your next steps.
- **Stay connected.** Maintain connections with your professional network. Relationships in the educational community can provide support and open doors to new opportunities.
- **Be open to new opportunities.** Embrace the change as a chance to explore new avenues in your career. Be open to roles and opportunities that you may not have considered before.
- **Prioritise self-care.** Transitions can be stressful. Prioritise your well-being through self-care practices, hobbies, or spending time with loved ones.
- **Seek support and guidance.** Don't hesitate to seek support from mentors, colleagues, or professional counsellors during this transition phase.
- **Realign your goals.** Use this period as an opportunity to realign your professional goals. What are your aspirations now? What new challenges do you want to take on?

In conclusion, embracing the future after moving on from a leadership role is a journey of self-discovery, resilience, and growth. It is about looking back with gratitude, looking forward with hope, and stepping into the next phase of your professional life with renewed purpose and enthusiasm. The transition may not be easy, but it is integral to your continuous journey as an educational leader.

11.7 Key takeaways

"I start with the premise that the function of leadership is to produce more leaders, not more followers." This quote is attributed to Ralph Nader, an American political activist, author, lecturer, and attorney. It encapsulates the idea that effective leadership is about empowering others to become leaders rather than simply amassing followers. Reflecting on my work as principal, I feel a sense of accomplishment in this space.

As I conclude this chapter, it is fitting to reflect on the journey of one of my deputy principals, later in my professional career, who epitomised the spirit of leadership and the enduring impact of mentorship. In the wake of my departure as principal, they seamlessly took up the torch, serving as the acting principal for a year. It was a period marked by their steadfast commitment and leadership, ensuring stability and continued growth for the school during its transition. Their tenure as acting principal was more than a mere placeholder; it was a testament to their capability and dedication to the school's ethos and its community.

In a move that demonstrated strategic foresight and judicious decision-making, my deputy made the thoughtful decision not to apply for the permanent principal position at our school. Instead, they looked further afield, a decision that spoke volumes about their confidence and readiness for broader challenges. This step led them to an extraordinary opportunity – being appointed as the head of the campus at one of the country's largest and finest multi-campus independent schools. Their ascent to this prestigious role was not just a personal triumph but also a reflection of the legacy we strive to leave in educational leadership, nurturing leaders who are not only capable of steering the ship in familiar waters but also daring enough to navigate new horizons.

This chapter has underscored the critical importance of thoughtful succession planning, the art of mentorship, and the impactful process of leaving a lasting legacy in educational leadership.

The journey of identifying and nurturing future leaders, as shared in these narratives, emphasises the role of mentorship as a foundational element in fostering leadership capabilities in others. It is about recognising potential, providing guidance, and setting the stage for the next generation of leaders. The preparation for leadership transition, both emotionally and practically, involves careful planning and a clear vision for the school's future, ensuring a seamless handover and continued success.

Moreover, leaving a legacy highlights a leader's enduring impact on their school and community. It reflects values, contributions, and the culture fostered during their tenure. As educational leaders, our legacy is woven into the fabric of the school's identity and the lives of those we have influenced.

As you reflect on your own leadership journey, consider the legacy you wish to leave behind. How will your actions and decisions today shape the future of your school and its community? Succession planning, mentorship, and legacy are responsibilities and opportunities to contribute to a sustainable and thriving educational environment. Embrace these opportunities and be mindful of the indelible mark you leave on the world of education.

CONCLUSION

As we draw the curtains on this exploration of principal leadership, it is fitting to reflect on the journey we have undertaken together. In these pages, we have traversed the multifaceted landscape of principal leadership, delving into the challenges and triumphs that define the role of a principal. As I think about this journey, I am reminded of Nelson Mandela's (1994) profound words: "It always seems impossible until it's done." This sentiment resonates deeply with the craft of my leadership – where challenges often seem insurmountable, yet the relentless spirit of a dedicated leader can pave the way to remarkable achievements.

Throughout my four decades of leadership in schools, with 24 years in the principalship across diverse settings, I have come to see this role as much more than a job; it is a calling. It is a vocation that demands not just intellectual acumen, but also emotional resilience, ethical fortitude, and a heart deeply invested in the future of our young learners. My journey, spanning various schools and states, has been a mosaic of experiences – each chapter in this book reflects those myriad encounters and learnings.

In each part of the book, from envisioning a compelling future for your school to managing crises and leading with ethical integrity, the goal has been to offer practical and transformative insights. The role of a principal is akin to being a captain navigating a ship through both calm and stormy seas. It requires a keen sense of direction, the ability to make tough decisions under pressure, and, most importantly, the capacity to inspire and motivate others to work towards a common goal.

One of the most critical aspects we have touched upon is the importance of leaving a legacy – the art of succession planning. "The true meaning of life is to plant trees, under whose shade you do not expect to sit" (Nelson Henderson). This quote encapsulates the idea of doing good deeds for the benefit of future generations, emphasising selflessness and long-term thinking. This aspect of leadership ensures that the values, vision, and efforts you have instilled continue to flourish long after you have passed the torch to the next leader.

Moreover, the balancing act of managing resources, priorities, and personal well-being cannot be overstated. Finding harmony between work and personal life is beneficial and essential in a profession where burnout is all too common. This balance sustains a leader's ability to perform effectively over the long haul.

Reflecting on my career, I see a path filled with opportunities to shape young minds, influence future leaders, and contribute meaningfully to the educational landscape. The joy of witnessing students' growth, staff development, and the flourishing of schools under effective leadership is unparalleled. This book is an invitation to embrace the role of principal with passion and purpose, to find fulfilment in the challenges and rewards it presents.

As you step forward in your leadership path, remember that your work is vital, impactful, and deeply valued. Keep forging ahead, for in the words of Mandela, "After climbing a great hill, one only finds that there are many more hills to climb."

The journey of leadership is continuous, filled with learning and growth at every turn. Embrace it enthusiastically, and may your legacy be as enriching and impactful as the journey itself.

In closing, this book is more than just a guide; it is an invitation to embark on a journey of leadership that is as challenging as it is rewarding. My hope is that these pages inspire you to embrace the role of principal with passion, perseverance, and a deep sense of purpose. May you find in your journey the same fulfilment and sense of accomplishment that I have found in mine.

REFERENCES

AITSL. (2024). *Improve with our coaching resources.* https://www.aitsl.edu.au/lead-develop/develop-others/coach-others/coaching-resources

Arnold, K. (1995). *Designing dispute resolution systems in schools.* Track Two. https://journals.co.za/doi/pdf/10.10520/AJA10197435_244

Bennett, W. (2009). *The Man in the Mirror.* Harper Collins.

Duffin, P. (2024, May 9). Student with knife sends Sydney school into lockdown, staff member injured. *Sydney Morning Herald.* https://www.smh.com.au/national/nsw/student-with-knife-sends-sydney-school-into-lockdown-staff-member-injured-20240509-p5jb8i.html

Fogarty EDvance. (2024). *Advancing educational opportunities.* https://fogartyedvance.au/

Independent Schools Australia (ISA). (2024). *Recurrent funding.* https://isa.edu.au/our-sector/funding/recurrent-funding/

Kerr, J. (2013). *Legacy: What the All Blacks Can Teach Us About the Business of Life.* Little Brown.

Mandela, N. (1994). *Long Walk to Freedom: The Autobiography of Nelson Mandela.* Little Brown.

Merchant, N. (2011). Culture trumps strategy, every time. *Harvard Business Review.* https://hbr.org/2011/03/culture-trumps-strategy-every-time

Panmore Institute. (2023). *Google's (Alphabet's) organizational culture & its traits.* https://panmore.com/google-organizational-culture-characteristics-analysis

Roberts, Phil. (2024). Feedback notes for the author's consideration. Personal communication.

Rosenberg, M. B. (2015). *Nonviolent Communication: A Language of Life: Life-Changing Tools for Healthy Relationships* (3rd Ed.). PuddleDancer Press.

www.ingramcontent.com/pod-product-compliance
Lightning Source LLC
Chambersburg PA
CBHW050352120526
44590CB00015B/1663